Popular Complete Smart Series

Complete

EnglishSmart®

Revised and Updated!

Grammar

Comprehension

Vocabulary

Writing

Usage

Grade **5**

Credits

Photo (Cover "children"/123RF.com)

ISBN: 978-1-897457-05-4

Complete EnglishSmart **Contents**

ISBN: 978-1-897457-05-4

ISBN: 978-1-897457-05-4

ISBN: 978-1-897457-05-4

ISBN: 978-1-897457-05-4

When a house cat sits on your lap purring, it is hard to believe that this cuddly, furry animal could belong to the same family as the sabre-toothed tiger. The first cat was likely the Miacis, a small weasel-like meat eater that dates back about 60 million years. The Miacis would not have resembled today's cat, as it was likely an ancestor of the dog and possibly the bear as well. The first cat-like ancestor, the Dinictis, dates back about 10 million years.

The early cat family was split into two <u>distinct</u> groups: the *sabre-toothed tigers* and *true cats*. The sabre-toothed tigers were big, <u>powerful</u> animals that roamed the Earth for nearly 35 million years. They have been <u>extinct</u> for nearly 12,000 years. The second group, true cats, can be further divided into three categories: big cats (lions, tigers, jaguars, leopards), small cats (felines), and cheetahs. The cheetah is in a <u>classification</u> of its own because it <u>developed</u> separately, becoming the fastest animal on Earth capable of speeds of up to 100 kph.

The small cat is a <u>broad</u> classification and includes the lynx, the bobcat, the cougar, and other similarly sized members.

Both big cats and small cats use similar <u>methods</u> of hunting. The leopard will <u>stalk</u> its prey and upon catching it, deliver a fatal bite to the back of the neck bringing quick death to its victim. Small cats, even domestic cats, are capable of similar hunting methods. A house cat will lie in waiting for an <u>unsuspecting</u> bird to land and then pounce on it or it may hold a mouse with its claws and deliver the fatal bite.

The 41 breeds of <u>domestic</u> cats are so <u>popular</u> that many have become <u>famous</u>. Among these superstar cats are Morris, the star of television commercials, Felix of cartoon fame, Dr. Seuss's Cat in the Hat, and Garfield.

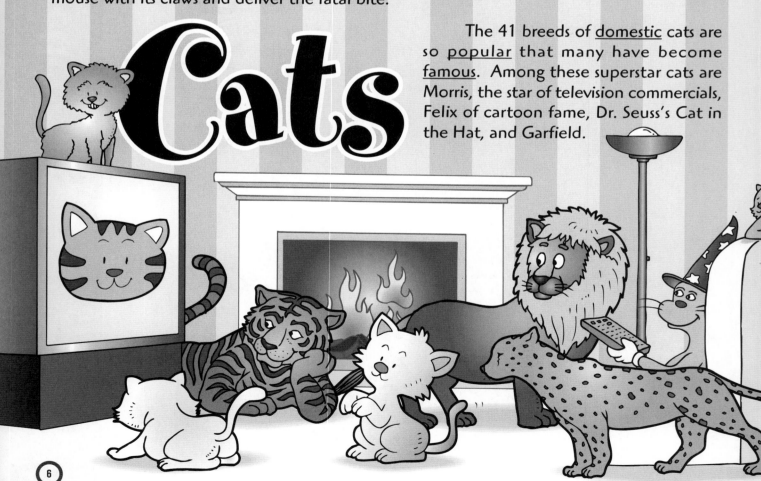

ISBN: 978-1-897457-05-4

Recalling Details

A.   For each statement, fill in the blank with the best fact from the choices given.

1.   The first cat dates back _____ years.

   30 million   60 million   5 million   250,000

2.   The first cat was a weasel-like meat eater called a _____ .

   Feline   Dinictis   Miacis   Sabre-toothed tiger

3.   The sabre-toothed tigers roamed the Earth for _____ years.

   35 million   80 million   100,000   500,000

4.   Sabre-toothed tigers have been extinct for _____ years.

   100,000   50,000   60,000   12,000

5.   Cats are divided into two main groups: _____ .

   fierce and tame   sabre-toothed tigers and true cats
   striped and plain   lions and tigers

6.   The _____ has its own classification.

   leopard   tiger   lion   cheetah

7.   The lynx, bobcat, and cougar are members of the _____ group.

   big cat   forest cat   small cat   fierce cat

8.   Both big cats and small cats are similar _____ .

   runners   hunters   breeds   pets

9.   There are _____ different kinds of domestic cats.

   85   104   41   14

10.   The fastest cat, clocked at up to 100 kph, is the _____ .

   cheetah   lion   lynx   panther

ISBN: 978-1-897457-05-4

Common and Proper Nouns

- **Common Nouns** *name non-specific persons, places, or things.*
  Examples : *house, girl, boy, dog, store, bicycle*

- **Proper Nouns** *name specific persons, places, or things.*
  Examples : *Atlantic Ocean, Christopher Columbus, Ontario Place*

B.   Underline the proper nouns and circle the common nouns in each sentence below.

There are 13 common nouns and 14 proper nouns.

1.   The tourists from Japan visited Niagara Falls and took the Maid of the Mist boat ride.

2.   Mr. Smith taught at Maple Road Public School for twenty years.

3.   The boys played soccer while the girls played baseball.

4.   Jenny and her friend Susan were in the school play, A Christmas Story.

5.   Don't step in the puddle by the bottom step.

6.   The CN Tower is one of the tallest structures in North America.

7.   Mr. Jones travelled to England and visited Buckingham Palace.

8.   We travelled across Europe by train.

ISBN: 978-1-897457-05-4

Words in Context

- **Context** refers to the meaning of the sentence in which a word is used. From the meaning of a sentence, we can understand the meanings of the unfamiliar words used in that sentence.

C.   Write the underlined words in the passage that match the meanings.

Meaning	Underlined Word
1. well-known	_____
2. unaware	_____
3. type	_____
4. no longer existing	_____
5. specific, special	_____
6. wide-ranging	_____
7. strong	_____
8. formed	_____
9. tame	_____
10. ways of doing things	_____
11. hunt	_____
12. well-liked	_____

ISBN: 978-1-897457-05-4

The "Horseless Carriage" (1)

Just <u>imagine</u> a world without the automobile. You would likely live in the city or town and be within walking distance of the things you need. Today, many people live in <u>suburbs</u> or in rural areas that, a hundred years ago, would have been considered too far from the everyday amenities. The <u>invention</u> of the automobile changed not only where people lived but also how they lived, and what they did with their leisure time.

The quest to replace the horse and carriage goes back to the early 1770s. Frenchman Joseph Cugnot built a steam-powered three-wheeler, but <u>critics</u> claimed that it was too slow and that it was no match for the horse. It wasn't until the 1850s that internal combustion engines <u>powered</u> by gas and air appeared on the scene. This was an <u>improvement</u> over the steam engine, but it was Nicholas Otto who <u>perfected</u> the internal combustion engine. His was light and efficient enough to be used in a transport vehicle. It <u>paved</u> the way for the swift <u>development</u> of the early automobile.

In 1865, Karl Benz, a German engineer, built the first <u>successful</u> gasoline-powered automobile. Like Cugnot's design, it was a three-wheeler, and with the Otto engine, it was <u>capable</u> of speeds of up to nine miles an hour. In 1890, Benz built a four-wheeled vehicle which he displayed in America. It was this automobile that <u>inspired</u> the Duryea brothers, originally <u>bicycle mechanics</u>, to build the first American-made automobile in 1893.

The first automobile to be sold in America was purchased in 1896 and the only thing that remained to be figured out was how to mass-produce it so that everyone could afford one. Once that was accomplished, there would be great changes in the American way of life.

ISBN: 978-1-897457-05-4

Fact or Opinion

- **Facts** *are based on exact information from the passage.* **Opinion** *is your personal view based on the facts from the passage.*

A.   Place "F" for fact or "O" for opinion beside each statement.

1. _____ Many people today live in suburbs.

2. _____ The effort to replace the horse and carriage began in the 1770s.

3. _____ Cugnot built a steam-powered three-wheeled vehicle.

4. _____ Most people like living in rural areas.

5. _____ Without the automobile, travel would not be as easy as it is today.

6. _____ The first gasoline-powered car was built by Karl Benz.

7. _____ Benz was lucky that he had the Otto engine to work with.

8. _____ Benz displayed his four-wheeled car in America.

9. _____ The Americans were impressed with the Benz car.

10. _____ The Duryea brothers were influenced by the Benz car.

11. _____ In 1896 the first automobile was sold in America.

12. _____ Mass production was necessary to make cars cheap enough for everyone.

Your Opinion

B.   Answer the questions.

1. Why do you think many people were hesitant to replace the horse and carriage with the automobile?

   _____

   _____

2. What was the most important advancement in developing the car?

   _____

   _____

ISBN: 978-1-897457-05-4

 **Verbs**

- **Verbs** are often action words. They tell what something or someone has done.
  Example: The boy jumped over the fence.
  In this case the verb is "jumped" since it tells what the boy did.

- Verbs are sometimes non-action words. They state that something exists or describe the state of the nouns.
  Example: The food is on the table.
  In this case the verb is "is". Notice that there is no real action here.

C. Write "A" if the verb is an action verb or "N" if it is a non-action verb.

1. The steam-powered three-wheeler was no match for the horse. _____
2. Karl Benz built the first gasoline-powered automobile. _____
3. The car sped down the street. _____
4. It then made a sharp turn and disappeared in no time. _____
5. The hockey player shot the puck into the net. _____
6. John is the tallest boy in the class. _____
7. The girls are in the school play. _____
8. Kitty will play Snow White. _____
9. The zookeeper feeds the animals at the same time every day. _____
10. He usually takes a rest in the late afternoon. _____

D. Complete the story with your own choice of verbs.

The students 1._____ in the schoolyard until the bell rang.

On hearing the bell, the teacher 2._____ them to come inside.

There 3._____ still a lot of noise in the hallway. Finally, they

4._____ quiet. The teacher 5._____ the students to

take out their notebooks and 6._____ the words on the board.

ISBN: 978-1-897457-05-4

Building New Words

- Most words have other forms depending on how they are used in a sentence. For example, if you want to make a noun out of the verb "divide", you would change it to "division".

  Here are some examples of new words that can be built from existing words:

  move – movement   associate – association
  final – finalize   begin – beginning

E. **For each case, find the underlined word in the passage that shares the same root with the word below.**

	Given Word	Underlined Word
1.	inspiration	
2.	capability	
3.	pavement	
4.	critical	
5.	inventor	
6.	imagination	
7.	develop	
8.	perfection	
9.	cycling	
10.	improve	
11.	success	
12.	powerful	
13.	suburban	
14.	mechanical	

ISBN: 978-1-897457-05-4

Although the first automobile was built in Germany, it was the Americans that figured out a way to <u>mass</u>-produce it. The goal was to build automobiles in such a way that it was cost-effective so that the money saved in <u>manufacturing</u> could be passed on to the consumers. As a result, there would be a reasonably priced car that everyone could <u>own</u>.

In 1893, Henry Ford built his first car based on the Benz model. Benz continued to build expensive cars in Europe for upper class purchasers. Ford had a better <u>idea</u>. He wanted to build cars for everyone. Ford visited a slaughterhouse and watched as the butchers cut the cattle up in an assembly line with each station chopping

The "Horseless Carriage" (2)

off a particular portion of beef. Ford decided to apply this method to the production of cars and the automobile assembly line was born – a method still used today.

In 1908, Ford produced the Model "T" which was a simple family car without the fancy <u>trappings</u> found on German cars. In 1913, he created his assembly line and the cars began to roll out. The more he produced, the lower the prices were until he managed to get the price of his Model "T" down to about $285.00. In 1914, Ford paid his workers an incredible $5.00 per day for wages. That was nearly twice the average wage for similar work at that time. Businessmen declared that this was a ridiculously <u>high</u> <u>wage</u> and that he would go broke. Ford reasoned that if he paid his <u>workers</u> enough money, they could afford to buy his cars. By 1924 Ford had sold 2 million cars.

Ford created mass production but it was General Motors that understood marketing. They introduced the yearly model change which enticed buyers to purchase the latest style of car. They also introduced the "payment plan" whereby a buyer could purchase a car on credit and make monthly payments. North Americans fell in love with the automobile and the freedom it created, and soon nearly every <u>household</u> in America owned a car.

ISBN: 978-1-897457-05-4

Cause and Effect

- An **Effect** is the result of something happening or of something being done. The **Cause** is what is happening or being done.

For example, in The "Horseless Carriage" (1), we could say that the invention of the automobile was a "cause" and the "effect" was that it changed the way people travelled.

A. **For each case below, you are given either a cause or an effect. Where you have a cause, give an effect and for an effect given, suggest a cause.**

1. Cause: _____

    _____

    Effect: Cars would be cheap enough for everyone to own.

2. Cause: Henry Ford visited a slaughterhouse.

    Effect: _____

    _____

3. Cause: _____

    _____

    Effect: The Model "T" dropped in price to $285.00.

4. Cause: _____

    _____

    Effect: Ford's workers could afford to buy his cars.

5. Cause: General Motors introduced the yearly model change.

    Effect: _____

    _____

6. Cause: _____

    _____

    Effect: Purchasers of the automobile could make monthly payments.

ISBN: 978-1-897457-05-4

Transitive and Intransitive Verbs

- A **Transitive Verb** must take an object.

  Example: The students need pencils. "Need" is a transitive verb because it requires an object which is the receiver of the verb.

- An **Intransitive Verb** does not need an object to receive the action of the verb.

  Example: The children played. "Played" is an intransitive verb because it is complete in its meaning and does not require an object.

B. Circle the verbs and write "T" for transitive verbs and "I" for intransitive verbs. Underline the objects of the verbs.

There are 7 intransitive verbs.

1. _____ Spectators lined the parade route.

2. _____ We watched the parade from the balcony.

3. _____ The marching band wore bright costumes.

4. _____ The horns played loudly.

5. _____ Clowns gave candy to the children.

6. _____ Everyone smiled at the dog in costume.

7. _____ The parade lasted for two hours.

8. _____ Most people stayed until the end.

9. _____ Jugglers tossed fiery torches into the air.

10. _____ Clouds filled the sky, threatening rain.

11. _____ The leader of the band smiled at everyone.

12. _____ Just as the rain started, the parade ended.

ISBN: 978-1-897457-05-4

Synonyms

- **Synonyms** are words that have similar meanings.

  Examples: large – big   tiny – small

  sad – upset   incredible – unbelievable

C. **Complete the crossword puzzle with the underlined synonyms from the passage for the clue words.**

Across

A. many
B. possess
C. extras
D. earnings

Down

1. home
2. making
3. thought
4. lofty
5. employees

ISBN: 978-1-897457-05-4

Influenza –
More Than Just a Cold

Typically during the winter months, many people come down with what is commonly called the "flu". The symptoms may be mild, like those associated with the common cold, or more severe. Often, the symptoms will include fever, chills, headache, and body aches. A person may feel aches in many of his or her joints and experience a loss of appetite.

Usually an influenza attack lasts from four days to two weeks, and although uncomfortable, it does not cause great harm. However, some influenza viruses can be more serious. The influenza virus, depending on the strain, can weaken the body to the point where pneumonia and other diseases can set in. In some cases, particularly for the elderly or people who are already very ill, the flu can be fatal.

From 1918 to 1919, a worldwide influenza epidemic killed 25 million people. This particular strain was one of the five deadliest epidemics of all time. But in 1918 there was no scientific treatment for the infection. Today, antibiotics can protect people from developing pneumonia and other diseases that can follow the flu. Doctors have developed vaccines that can protect people against flu viruses. The problem is that the strains of flu are constantly changing and it is difficult for doctors to keep up with the new influenzas that spread around the world.

The concern over influenza is so great that The Centre for Disease Control and Prevention (CDC) has created a special department to stay on alert to report any new strains of flu the moment they arise. Today, doctors are encouraging people to take flu shots. Although flu shots may not prevent the flu, they could significantly lessen the impact of the virus. Health care workers, the elderly, and people with chronic illnesses are encouraged to get their flu shots first.

ISBN: 978-1-897457-05-4

Recalling Details

A. **Fill in the blanks with the appropriate words or numbers from the list provided.**

| fever | vaccines | illnesses | antibiotics | 5 | CDC |
| 25 | appetite | flu | pneumonia | shots | elderly |

The word 1._____ is often used as a short form of the word influenza. Symptoms of influenza may include aches, chills, and 2._____ . A person with influenza may experience a loss of 3._____ . Severe influenza viruses may lead to 4._____ or other diseases. A worldwide influenza epidemic in 1919 caused 5._____ million deaths, making this epidemic in the top 6._____ of all-time deadly epidemics. 7._____ are used today to fight against the development of more serious diseases. To protect people against viruses, scientists have developed 8._____ but these have to change with each new strain. The 9._____ created a special department to deal with all the new viral strains. There are influenza 10._____ available to the general public to control influenza. Health care workers, the 11._____ , and people with chronic 12._____ should protect themselves against influenza.

B. **Answer the following questions.**

1. What is the biggest problem the medical community faces today regarding influenza?

    _____

    _____

2. Who are most at risk of serious illness brought on by influenza and why is this so?

    _____

    _____

Direct and Indirect Objects

- A **Direct Object** is the receiver of the action of the verb.
  Example: The boy rode the bicycle.
  "Bicycle" is the direct object of the verb because it directly receives the action of the verb.

- An **Indirect Object** answers the question to whom the action of the verb is directed.
  Example: The father gave his son a birthday gift.
  The "son" is the indirect object because he is the person to whom the giving was done. The "gift" would be the direct object because it was the thing that was given.

C. State whether each underlined object is direct "D" or indirect "I".

1. The players wore <u>sweaters</u> for the game. _____

2. People who live in the forest cut <u>trees</u> for shelter. _____

3. The mother told her <u>daughter</u> stories about her youth. _____

4. He gave <u>her</u> a ride to school. _____

5. He asked the <u>person</u> in front of him to move over. _____

6. They gave the charity a lot of <u>money</u>. _____

7. The father read his <u>son</u> a bedtime story. _____

8. The library showed the <u>children</u> films on Saturday. _____

D. Use these words to complete the paragraph.

trip	way	he	bicycle	drink
	top	bottom	hill	

Michael rode his <u>1._____</u> up the <u>2._____</u> . When <u>3._____</u> reached the <u>4._____</u> , he was very tired. He took a <u>5._____</u> from his water bottle and put it back in his knapsack. The <u>6._____</u> back down was much easier as he coasted all the <u>7._____</u> to the <u>8._____</u> .

ISBN: 978-1-897457-05-4

Words Often Confused

- *Some words have similar spelling patterns and sounds even though their meanings might be quite different.*

E. Select the appropriate word for each sentence based on the definitions given below. Underline your choice.

accept	to receive	addition	something added
except	to be left out	edition	published copies
stationary	not moving	adapt	to adjust to something
stationery	things for writing	adept	to be good at doing something
berth	a place to sleep	role	a part a character plays
birth	being born	roll	to turn about
lay	to put down	miner	one who works in a mine
lie	to sit back	minor	one under a legal age
council	a group	altar	a place of worship
counsel	legal advice	alter	to change

1. The boy went up to (accept, except) his award.

2. He read the first (addition, edition) of the school yearbook.

3. The high priest placed the sacrifice on the (alter, altar).

4. The girl was (adept, adapt) at reading and writing.

5. For the long trip, they ordered a (birth, berth) on the train.

6. The (counsel, council) members met once a month.

7. (Lie, Lay) the tablecloth in preparation for dinner.

8. The (miner, minor) was not allowed to buy cigarettes.

9. In the school play, he played the (role, roll) of the villain.

10. The (stationary, stationery) remained (stationary, stationery) on the desk.

In the 13th century, trade between Europe and Asia was channelled through the "Silk Route", the trade route from China to Constantinople (now Istanbul). The Muslims controlled and restricted trade with the East and the merchants of the Mediterranean were completely cut off from the established trade route. The European merchants wanted the silk, spices, and gold found in the East. So important was this market that the Europeans were willing to go to great expense and trouble to find new trade routes.

The Polo family, merchants from Venice, made the trip to China which was part of a fourteen-year excursion. Their objective was to bring back marketable goods to be sold in Venice. At the request of the Chinese ruler, the great Kublai Kahn, they were to return to China and bring with them many learned men. Kublai Kahn was interested in learning about the European culture.

The Polo family set out for China in 1271 for what was to be a four-year journey. They crossed Asia Minor (Turkey) and Persia (present-day Iran and Iraq). They stayed for nearly a

Treasures
of the Orient (1)

year in northern Afghanistan likely because of illness. Their journey took them across the Himalayan mountains and the Gobi desert and finally to Shangdu (present-day Beijing) where they were reunited with Kublai Kahn.

The Polos stayed in China for another 17 years and became very wealthy. Marco Polo recorded the events of his travels in a book that told of the riches of the Orient. It was his book that inspired Europeans to share in the wealth by finding a trade route by water that would be quick and profitable. The race to discover a trade route was officially launched.

ISBN: 978-1-897457-05-4

Recalling Information

A. Write "T" for true statements and "F" for false ones.

1. Europe and Asia once traded through the Silk Route.   _____

2. The Polo family were traders from Rome, Italy.   _____

3. European merchants wanted to sell silk and spices.   _____

4. The Polos made a trip to Asia that lasted 14 years.   _____

5. Kublai Kahn was a famous European leader.   _____

6. Persia was today's Iran and Iraq.   _____

7. The Polos were not interested in trading goods.   _____

8. The Polos travelled across the Himalayan mountains.   _____

9. Marco Polo recorded the events of his travels in a book.   _____

10. Polo's book was not interesting to Europeans.   _____

11. Kublai Kahn was not interested in European culture.   _____

12. Istanbul was formerly known as Constantinople.   _____

Making Assumptions

B. Answer the questions.

1. Why were Europeans interested in establishing a new trade route by water?

_____

_____

2. What do you think the Europeans could offer for trade in the Orient?

_____

_____

Unit 5

Subject Pronouns

- A **Subject Pronoun** acts as a subject of a sentence by taking the place of the subject noun.

  Examples: Susan likes eating cake.   She likes eating cake.

  The boys played football.   They played football.

  Note: If the noun being replaced by the pronoun is plural, the pronoun must be plural.

C.   Replace the subject nouns with pronouns.

1.   The students were late for class. _____ were late for class.

2.   John ate his lunch alone. _____ ate his lunch alone.

3.   My friend and I watched television. _____ watched television.

4.   Susan wore her new coat. _____ wore her new coat.

Object Pronouns

- An **Object Pronoun** can replace a noun as both a **Direct** and an **Indirect Object**.

  Example 1: Rachel was a new student in the school. The students welcomed her.

  The pronoun "her" replaces the noun, Rachel. Since the pronoun directly receives the action of the verb "welcomed", it is a pronoun as direct object.

  Example 2: Rachel was a new student in the school. The students gave her a warm welcome.

  The pronoun "her" is the indirect object because Rachel was the person to whom the welcome was given.

D.   For each statement, underline the object pronoun and place the word "Direct" or "Indirect" in the space.

1.   Paul gave me the books to read.   _____

2.   The students threw him up in the air in celebration.   _____

3.   I told him my name.   _____

4.   His friends took him out for dinner on his birthday.   _____

5.   Give her the money.   _____

ISBN: 978-1-897457-05-4

Word Meanings

E. **The words in Column A appear in the reading passage. Match them with the meanings in Column B.**

Column A	Column B
1. channelled	A. cost
2. established	B. to ask for
3. expense	C. sent in one direction
4. excursion	D. heritage
5. objective	E. encouraged
6. request	F. made, developed
7. culture	G. trip
8. inspired	H. purpose

Using New Words

F. **Write a sentence of your own using the two new words.**

1. excursion, objective

_____

_____

2. channelled, expense

_____

_____

3. established, culture

_____

_____

4. inspired, request

_____

_____

ISBN: 978-1-897457-05-4

Europe in the mid-fifteenth century was eager to establish trade routes by sea to the Far East. They were anxious to bring in exotic goods such as gold, silk, and spices that could be sold at home for great profits.

Portuguese explorers were preparing to sail around Africa in search of a trade route. Christopher Columbus had another idea. He believed that the Earth was round and therefore by sailing west, he would eventually reach the Orient. Sponsored by Queen Isabella and King Ferdinand of Spain, he set sail in 1492 with three ships and a crew of 90 men. It is likely that Columbus first landed in one of the Bahama Islands. Columbus named the area the Indies, which came to be known as the West Indies. Columbus did not discover the route to the Orient. Instead, he discovered the Americas (now America).

Treasures
of the Orient (2)

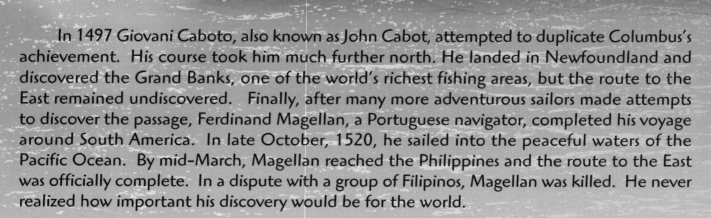

In 1497 Giovani Caboto, also known as John Cabot, attempted to duplicate Columbus's achievement. His course took him much further north. He landed in Newfoundland and discovered the Grand Banks, one of the world's richest fishing areas, but the route to the East remained undiscovered. Finally, after many more adventurous sailors made attempts to discover the passage, Ferdinand Magellan, a Portuguese navigator, completed his voyage around South America. In late October, 1520, he sailed into the peaceful waters of the Pacific Ocean. By mid-March, Magellan reached the Philippines and the route to the East was officially complete. In a dispute with a group of Filipinos, Magellan was killed. He never realized how important his discovery would be for the world.

Thanks to the interest sparked by Marco Polo's book and the navigational skill of Magellan, two routes to the riches of the Orient were discovered – one in the east and the other in the west.

ISBN: 978-1-897457-05-4

Drawing Conclusions

A. Answer the questions.

1. Why did Europeans think that trade with the Orient would be profitable?

_____

_____

2. Why were sailors attempting two different routes?

_____

_____

3. Why was Columbus's discovery of the Americas important?

_____

_____

4. Was John Cabot a successful explorer? Why?

_____

_____

5. What was the success of Magellan's voyage?

_____

_____

6. What was more important, the discovery of the Americas or finding the route to the Orient?

_____

_____

7. State who was the more successful explorer, Columbus or Magellan, and explain why.

_____

_____

ISBN: 978-1-897457-05-4

Possessive Adjectives

- **Possessive Adjectives** can replace nouns and express ownership.
  His, her, their, our, your, and my are examples.

B. Complete the sentences with suitable possessive adjectives.

1. Bill and Jean found _____ home in the suburbs.

2. The boy lost _____ keys when he opened _____ school bag.

3. We are proud of what _____ children have accomplished.

4. You must check _____ name on the voter's list.

5. Susan was happy with _____ report card.

6. The barefooted boy said, "I've left _____ shoes in the car."

Relative Pronouns

- **Relative Pronouns** refer to nouns or pronouns that precede them which are called
  Antecedents.

  Example 1: John, who is ten, is in grade five.
  The pronoun "who" refers to the antecedent noun, "John".

  Example 2: The store, which is located in the plaza, was closed.
  The pronoun "which" refers to the antecedent noun, "store".

  Example 3: He caught the ball that was tossed to him.
  The pronoun "that" refers to the antecedent noun, "ball".

  Note: "Who" and "whom" refer to people; "which" refers to things and animals;
  "that" refers to any antecedent.

C. For each case, choose the appropriate relative pronoun.

1. Paul, which, who _____ is the eldest child in the family, must take care of his little sister.

2. The game, whom, which _____ is played using a game board, was enjoyed by the children.

3. We played with the dog that, who _____ belonged to our neighbour.

4. The boy to whom, which _____ the prize was given was very happy.

ISBN: 978-1-897457-05-4

Word Search Challenge

D. Unscramble the words from the reading passage and place the corresponding letters in the spaces provided.

1. ☐ o ☐ ☐ e ☐
   utoser (ways of going)

2. ☐ i ☐ p ☐ t ☐
   spetudi (argument)

3. ☐ r ☐ f ☐ ☐
   tiforp (gains)

4. e ☐ ☐ o ☐ ☐ ☐
   coexit (strange, different)

5. ☐ o ☐ ☐ g ☐
   evagoy (sailing trip)

> Use some of the new words you have learned from the passage.

E. Imagine that you are a cabin boy working on Magellan's ship. Write a letter home describing your adventure.

October 1, 1520

Dear _____ ,

_____

_____

_____

_____

_____

_____

_____

Yours truly,

ISBN: 978-1-897457-05-4

Gypsies — an Endangered Culture

When we use the term "endangered", we are usually referring to endangered species of animals. There is great concern over the many types of animals that are at risk of extinction. There are, however, many cultural groups that face extinction, one of which is the Gypsies of Europe.

The Gypsies originated in India and settled in Europe over 600 years ago. They were nomadic people, that is, they were constantly on the move from one country to another. They preferred not to take on steady work but chose temporary work on farms, in construction, or in sales. They lived in caravans rather than homes because caravans are mobile. Originally they were horse traders, but today most of this trading is done within their group and is not a money-making occupation. Gypsy women traditionally made objects like clothespins to sell while others were fortune-tellers.

The Eastern European Gypsies were more settled than those in Western Europe. These Gypsies often lived a stabler life in villages. They were entertainers and tradesmen who wore distinctive colourful clothing. Eating together is considered a sign of friendship by Gypsies. They are very conscious of cleanliness, separating their water for cooking from that used for washing and personal hygiene.

The Gypsies are becoming extinct because of assimilation. Many of the younger members of this culture are moving into the mainstream culture. Traditionally, Gypsies have been mistrusted by many people who think of them as dishonest in business. In the past, the work they did was useful and appreciated by society in general. Today, Gypsies are not welcome in many countries. In some places, they face hostility and oppression. As a result, many young Gypsies have chosen to join the cultures of the countries they inhabit.

ISBN: 978-1-897457-05-4

The Main Idea

- The **Main Idea** of a paragraph is a summary of what the writer is trying to convey to the reader.

A. **In one sentence, write the main idea of each paragraph in the space provided.**

Paragraph One

_____

_____

Paragraph Two

_____

_____

Paragraph Three

_____

_____

Paragraph Four

_____

_____

Drawing Conclusions

B. **Briefly state your answer to each of the following questions based on your understanding of the passage.**

1. Why do some people not like the Gypsies?

_____

_____

2. Why are the Gypsies becoming an extinct culture?

_____

_____

3. Why were the Gypsies thought to be colourful people?

_____

_____

ISBN: 978-1-897457-05-4

Adjectives and Adverbs

- **Adjectives** describe nouns. They might tell you how big, how many, what kind, or what colour a noun is.

- **Adverbs** describe verbs. They often give a detail about the verb in a sentence, such as how an action was done. Adverbs can also describe adjectives or other adverbs.

  Example: The girl ran. (with no descriptive words)

  The young girl ran swiftly. (with an adjective and adverb added)

C.   In the following sentences, underline the adjectives and circle the adverbs.

1.   The long train slowly crossed the highway delaying all the cars.

2.   The happy child enthusiastically opened her Christmas gifts.

3.   The disappointed children sat quietly at their desks.

4.   A loud voice rang out from the crowd.

5.   The rock band played loudly for their devoted fans.

D.   Add adjectives and adverbs to make the sentences more interesting.

1.   The boys swam in the lake.

_____

2.   The car moved down the road.

_____

3.   The lights of the building were shining.

_____

4.   The man sat in the park.

_____

ISBN: 978-1-897457-05-4

Descriptive Language

- Vivid, colourful language helps the reader visualize people, places, and things that you are describing.

E. **Replace the underlined words with more descriptive words from the list below.**

| spacious | thrilled | delicious | stormy | scampered |

1. They played football on a <u>big</u> field. _____

2. The weather was <u>bad</u>. _____

3. They were <u>glad</u> to be invited to the party. _____

4. He <u>ran</u> the length of the basketball court. _____

5. It was a <u>good</u> birthday cake. _____

F. **Fill in the blanks with the descriptive words provided.**

| steaming | poured | terrified | gleamed | abandoned | drenched | stormy |
| howled | tightly | skipped | patiently | flashed | booming | subside | arrived |

It was a 1._____ day and the wind 2._____ through the trees. The girl held on 3._____ to her little brother's hand as he was 4._____ of the lightning that 5._____ across the sky. Suddenly, after a 6._____ clap of thunder, rain 7._____ down on them. They ran for cover in an 8._____ shack by the roadside. There they waited 9._____ for the storm to 10._____ . Before long, the storm ended and the sun 11._____ from the clear sky. Happily the brother and sister 12._____ down the road on their way home. When they 13._____ home, they removed their 14._____ clothing and drank 15._____ hot chocolate.

Helen Keller, born in 1880 in Alabama, USA, would have likely been a very ordinary child if it were not for a sudden illness. At the age of just 18 months, she lost both her sight and her hearing. Later, this illness claimed her ability to speak as well. She had virtually no means of communicating with the outside world.

Distressed and frustrated, Helen grew up to become an unruly child who threw terrible tantrums out of frustration. She became completely uncontrollable – like a wild animal.

The Kellers tried to get help from different doctors but no one could suggest a method of treatment. The Kellers then met Anne Sullivan who agreed to move into the Keller home and teach Helen. The first thing Anne did was discipline Helen. She refused to allow her to eat without using a spoon and, despite her wild tantrums, refused to give in to Helen. She then moved into a cottage with Helen and continued her training without any outside interference.

The Amazing
Helen Keller (1)

Anne created codes of communication by tapping on the back of Helen's hand to represent words. Helen tapped back but didn't really understand what she was doing. One morning, when Anne and Helen were pumping water from the well, Anne spelled out the word "water" in the tapping code. At the same time, to reinforce the connection between the tapping and the actual water, Anne poured cold water over Helen's hand. Suddenly, a strange look came over Helen's face. Miraculously, she began to understand. She had finally made the connection that Anne had been striving to achieve. Helen became starved for information. Frantically, she touched everything around her learning new words. The connection to the outside world had finally been re-established. Anne had brought Helen out of the darkness.

ISBN: 978-1-897457-05-4

Referring to Facts

A. **Place a check mark in the circle that matches the best supporting fact for each statement.**

1. Anne came up with a way to communicate with Helen.

   (A) She spoke loudly in her ear.

   (B) She tapped the back of her hand.

   (C) She helped Helen draw pictures of objects.

2. Helen was frustrated with her disability.

   (A) Helen became very quiet.

   (B) Helen tried very hard to cooperate.

   (C) Helen threw tantrums like a wild animal.

3. The breakthrough in learning for Helen came one day.

   (A) They were pumping water.

   (B) Suddenly she could hear again.

   (C) Helen nearly drowned.

4. Helen's disability was a coincidence.

   (A) Helen had a childhood illness.

   (B) Helen had a serious accident.

   (C) Helen was born with her disability.

5. Anne was a strict teacher and disciplinarian.

   (A) Anne was cruel to Helen.

   (B) Anne refused to give in to Helen's tantrums.

   (C) Anne used severe punishment to train Helen.

6. There was no medical solution for Helen's problems.

   (A) Helen took medication for her disability.

   (B) Her family doctor suggested many methods of cure.

   (C) Doctors did not have an answer for Helen's parents.

ISBN: 978-1-897457-05-4

Unit 8

The Sentence and Its Parts

A sentence is made up of two parts: **Subject** and **Predicate**.

- The subject of a sentence is the person, thing, or idea being talked about in the sentence. It usually performs the action of the verb.
  Example: The boy fell down.
  "The boy" is the subject of the sentence. The bare subject is "boy".

- The predicate is the action (verb) in the sentence.
  Example: The boy fell down.
  "Fell down" is the predicate. The bare predicate (verb) is "fell", the action in the sentence.

B. **In each sentence below, separate the subject and the predicate with a vertical line.**

1. The boys and girls played in the yard.

2. Cats and dogs are not always friends.

3. Morning is my favourite time of day.

4. The wind howled through the night.

5. Summer holidays will be here soon.

C. **Circle the bare subject and underline the bare predicate in each of the following sentences.**

The bare subject of one of these sentences involves more than one word.

1. Getting to school on time was impossible for him.

2. The team arrived late for their game.

3. The waves crashed to the shore in the wind.

4. Happiness is eating ice cream.

5. Track and field athletes are a special breed.

ISBN: 978-1-897457-05-4

Similes

- A **Simile** is a comparison of two things that have some characteristics in common. The word "like" or "as" is used to join the two things that are being compared.
  Examples: He jumped like a rabbit.
  She was as snug as a bug.

D.   Complete each sentence by creating a simile comparison.

1.   She moved like a _____ in the water.

2.   He leaped like a _____ over the fence.

3.   The building towered like a _____ .

4.   The plane soared like a _____ .

5.   The moon was like a _____ in the sky.

6.   The sun shone like a _____ on fire.

7.   She slept like a _____ .

8.   Be quiet as a _____ when you come in the house.

9.   The cake was as flat as a _____ .

Personification

- **Personification** is a descriptive technique in which non-human things are given human characteristics.
  Examples: The sun kissed the flowers.
  The wind whispered to the trees.

E.   Fill in the blanks with words that personify. Choose appropriate words from the list provided.

crouched
whistled   kissed
laughed   protected
danced   called
waved   smiled

1.   The sun _____ at the flowers.

2.   The birds _____ a happy tune.

3.   The mountain _____ the trees from the wind.

4.   The bushes _____ in the howling wind.

5.   The hyenas _____ at their prey.

ISBN: 978-1-897457-05-4

The day that Helen first recognized the meaning of the word "water" marked the most critical turning point in her life. She became a dedicated and enthusiastic learner increasing her vocabulary daily. Anne, who was experienced in teaching the Braille system of reading for blind people, taught Helen to read using this method. Her progress from this point was truly amazing.

The Amazing
Helen Keller (2)

She learned to write with a specially designed typewriter. By the age of ten, she had learned to speak and to read by touching others' lips after only one month of training. At the age of twenty, she successfully completed the entrance examination to Radcliffe College. Helen graduated with honours four years later. Remarkably, she specialized in foreign languages and philosophy.

Helen's determination to make a profound contribution to the world did not stop with her personal accomplishments. She became a writer, completing her autobiography in 1903. She was determined to help the handicapped and served on the Massachusetts Commission for the Blind. Throughout her life, she was involved in fundraising for The American Institute for the Blind. She toured England, France, Egypt, Africa, Japan, Italy, and Australia as a speaker and lecturer on behalf of the handicapped. After World War II, she visited wounded American soldiers and helped maintain morale among them.

Helen Keller completed six more books for a total of seven in all. In 1955 she wrote *Teacher: Anne Sullivan Macy*, a dedication to her teacher, Anne Sullivan. In 1959, an American author, William Gibson, wrote *The Miracle Worker*, a play about Helen's life. This play was made into a major motion picture in 1962.

Helen Keller's story is an inspirational account of the incredible courage of a young girl.

ISBN: 978-1-897457-05-4

Finding Important Information

A. **Copy the exact words from the story that prove that each statement below is correct.**

1. The incident with the water was very important to Helen.

   _____

   _____

2. Helen was a successful author.

   _____

   _____

3. Helen's story inspired Hollywood moviemakers.

   _____

   _____

4. Helen helped many blind and disabled people.

   _____

   _____

5. Anne knew all about teaching blind people how to read.

   _____

   _____

6. Helen was able to get a university education.

   _____

   _____

7. Helen was not only able to learn English.

   _____

   _____

8. With her work, Helen travelled outside the United States.

   _____

   _____

ISBN: 978-1-897457-05-4

Building a Simple Sentence

- A **Simple Sentence** is made up of a subject, a predicate, and often descriptive words describing the subject and predicate.

  Here is a group of words that, when properly arranged, would make up a sentence that makes sense.

  Example: water / stepped / the / silly / into / child / muddy / the

  The silly child stepped into the muddy water.

  It would not make sense to say that "The muddy child stepped into the silly water".
  Nor would it be proper to say that "The silly water stepped into the muddy child".

B. **Rearrange the following groups of words into sentences that make sense. Circle the bare subject and underline the bare predicate (verb).**

Keep the adjectives (words that describe nouns) and the adverbs (words that describe verbs) close to the words they are describing.

1. store   at   the   bought   candy   children   the   the

    _____

2. racing   the   track   the   roared   cars   around

    _____

3. ice   the   careful   slipping   be   of   on

    _____

4. the   steaming   boy   pizza   hot   hungry   ate   the

    _____

5. water   colourful   drifted   the   across   sailboat   calm   the

    _____

ISBN: 978-1-897457-05-4

Prefixes and Suffixes

- A **Prefix** is an addition to the front of a word; a **Suffix** is added to the end of the word. Adding a prefix or a suffix to a root word forms a new word. In some cases an opposite meaning is created. In other cases there is a change in the form of the root word.

Examples: When the prefix "un" is added to "happy", a new word "unhappy", which has an opposite meaning, is created.

When the suffix "ness" is added to the word "happy", the adjective is changed to a noun "happiness".

C. Write the root word of each of the given words.

1. inappropriate _____

2. unkind _____

3. misspelled _____

4. inability _____

5. firmness _____

6. incomplete _____

D. Create a new word for each root word by adding either a prefix or a suffix below.

Some suffixes and prefixes may be used more than once.

un	im	able	in
ous	ation	ful	dis

1. help _____

2. possible _____

3. love _____

4. form _____

5. afraid _____

6. nerve _____

7. move _____

8. clear _____

9. agree _____

10. prove _____

11. truth _____

12. fame _____

13. crease _____

14. tend _____

ISBN: 978-1-897457-05-4

Comprehension: Recalling Facts

A.   Circle the letters of the correct answers.

1.   The fastest member of the cat family is the
   A. cheetah.   B. cougar.   C. snow leopard.
   D. sabre-toothed tiger.

2.   One of the following is not a member of the cat family:
   A. lynx   B. lion   C. jaguar   D. weasel

3.   Both big cats and small cats use similar methods of
   A. eating.   B. sleeping.   C. running.   D. hunting.

4.   The efforts to develop the automobile go back to the early
   A. 1600s.   B. 1770s.   C. 1920s.   D. 1840s.

5.   In 1865 a successful gas-powered car was built by
   A. Karl Benz.   B. Henry Ford.   C. Joseph Gugnot.
   D. Nicholas Otto.

6.   The first gas-powered automobile was capable of speeds of up to
   A. 50 mph.   B. 95 mph.   C. 9 mph.   D. 22 mph.

7.   Cars became available to everyone because of
   A. cheaper materials.   B. mass production.
   C. better wages.   D. competition.

8.   Ford got the idea for an assembly line from
   A. Karl Benz.   B. his wife.   C. a bicycle shop.
   D. a slaughterhouse.

9.   The first American car for the people was the
   A. Cadillac.   B. Model T.   C. Mercedes Benz.
   D. Ford pickup truck.

10.   The symptoms of the flu do not include
   A. body aches.   B. insomnia.
   C. loss of appetite.   D. headache.

ISBN: 978-1-897457-05-4

11. The number of people that died from the worldwide flu epidemic in 1919 was

    A. 50 million.   B. 5 million.

    C. 25 million.   D. 100 million.

12. To fight against flu viruses, doctors invented

    A. syrups.   B. Tylenol.   C. vaccines.   D. pills.

13. Marco Polo's greatest contribution was

    A. finding a route to America.

    B. climbing the Himalayas.

    C. writing a book about his travels.

    D. renaming Constantinople Istanbul.

14. Christopher Columbus was sponsored by

    A. King Henry.   B. Louis XIV.   C. Queen Isabella.

    D. the English nobility.

15. Magellan was killed

    A. by pirates.   B. in a storm.   C. by his own men.

    D. in the Philippines.

16. Gypsies originated in

    A. America.   B. England.   C. India.   D. China.

17. Gypsies are becoming extinct because of

    A. disease.   B. famine.   C. assimilation.

    D. overcrowding.

18. Helen Keller first learned to communicate through

    A. touch.   B. sound.   C. smell.   D. hearing.

19. Helen Keller became

    A. an artist.   B. a nurse.   C. a writer and speaker.

    D. a college professor.

20. The play and the film about Keller's life was titled

    A. The Keller Story.   B. The Keller Miracle.

    C. The Miracle Worker.   D. Anne and Helen.

ISBN: 978-1-897457-05-4

Verbs and Objects

> A direct object is the receiver of the action of the verb.

B. **In each sentence, write "T" if the underlined verb is transitive or "I" if it is intransitive. Circle the direct object.**

1. The morning dewdrops <u>soaked</u> the flowers in the garden. _____

2. The spider <u>trapped</u> the fly in its web. _____

3. The apples <u>fell</u> on the grass. _____

4. The football fans <u>left</u> the arena disappointedly. _____

5. The player <u>kicked</u> the ball into the net. _____

Pronouns

C. **Underline the pronoun in each sentence. Write "S" if it is a subject, "D" for a direct object, or "I" for an indirect object.**

1. She wore winter boots to school _____

2. The parents committee asked her to help raise funds. _____

3. The soccer ball hit him and a goal was prevented. _____

4. They were late for the movie. _____

5. Ashley gave him an interesting storybook. _____

Possessive Adjectives and Relative Pronouns

D. **Fill in the blanks with the correct possessive adjectives or relative pronouns.**

1. Paul brought _____ dog to school.

2. We warmed _____ hands on the radiator.

3. The players wore _____ uniforms with pride.

4. She always helps _____ mom do the chores.

5. You should keep _____ room clean and tidy.

ISBN: 978-1-897457-05-4

6.   The lady _____ I talked to on the bus is my neighbour.

7.   The CD _____ was on the desk is missing.

8.   The man _____ gave me the parcel is Mr. Robson.

Adjectives and Adverbs

E.   Underline the adjectives and circle the adverbs in the passage.

It was a cold and windy winter morning. The frozen streets were dangerously slippery. The delivery truck moved slowly down the icy street stopping cautiously in front of the grocery store. The driver stepped gently onto the sidewalk and held the car door tightly, cleverly avoiding a slip on the first step.

The Sentence and Its Parts

F.   Use a vertical line to divide each sentence into subject and predicate. Circle the bare subject and underline the bare predicate (verb).

1.   The cat chased the dog around the yard.

2.   The moon shone brightly in the night sky.

3.   Happiness is skiing down a mountain.

4.   He fell down on the slippery road.

5.   The students cheered their track and field team to victory.

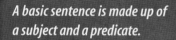

A basic sentence is made up of a subject and a predicate.

Building Sentences

G.   Rearrange the given words to create proper sentences.

1.   sports   his   soccer   favourite   were   hockey   and

_____

ISBN: 978-1-897457-05-4

2. blue was calm water sky was the and the

_____

3. day school were awards the given on out last of

_____

4. inside the for shelter rain he stop to the waited

_____

Recalling New Words

H. **Match the words from the passages with the synonyms.**

> extinct   domestic   stalk   critical   unsuspecting
> inspired   excursion   objective   exotic   broad

SYNONYMS

1. spacious _____
2. non-existent _____
3. hunt _____
4. unusual _____
5. serious _____
6. tame _____
7. trip _____
8. purpose _____
9. encouraged _____
10. innocent _____

Prefixes and Suffixes

I. **Create a new word for each root word by adding a prefix or a suffix.**

> un   im   able   in   ous   ation   ful   dis

1. possible _____
2. success _____
3. complete _____
4. transport _____

ISBN: 978-1-897457-05-4

5. fair _____   6. reason _____

7. fame _____   8. appear _____

Descriptive Language

J. **Choose a more vivid descriptive word from the word bank below that has the same meaning as the word in the list.**

exit   hazardous   scurried   fluffy   steaming   towering   firm
stroll   strike   enormous   attractive   agreeable   extensive   swift

1. big _____   2. pretty _____

3. nice _____   4. fast _____

5. long _____   6. high _____

7. unsafe _____ 8. soft _____

9. hard _____   10. leave _____

11. hot _____   12. walk _____

13. ran _____   14. hit _____

Composing Descriptive Sentences

cheerfully   loudly
swiftly   athletic
ferocious   speedy
angry   vicious   happy

K. **Add an adjective and adverb from the word bank to each sentence to create more interesting sentences.**

1. The dog barked.

_____

2. The girls ran.

_____

3. The crowd yelled.

_____

ISBN: 978-1-897457-05-4

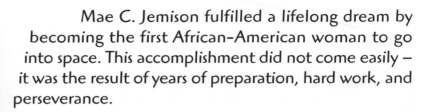

Mae C. Jemison fulfilled a lifelong dream by becoming the first African-American woman to go into space. This accomplishment did not come easily – it was the result of years of preparation, hard work, and perseverance.

Jemison was born on October 17, 1956 in Decatur, Alabama, and was the youngest of three children. Thanks to one of her uncles, who introduced her to the world of science, Jemison developed interests in anthropology, archaeology, and astronomy at an early age. In 1977, she graduated from Stanford University with degrees in chemical engineering and Afro-American studies. She earned a medical degree from Cornell University in 1981. The following year,

Mae Jemison –
a Great Inspiration

Jemison was selected by NASA (National Aeronautics and Space Administration) with 14 others to undergo astronaut training. Then in 1987, she was accepted into NASA's astronaut program, ready for the space mission. On September 12, 1992, her dream was finally realized. She flew on Space Shuttle Endeavour as the Mission Specialist and spent eight days in space before returning to Earth on September 20, 1992.

Jemison is a compassionate person. She has worked as a volunteer providing medical service in a Cambodian refugee camp and as a medical officer with the Peace Corps in West Africa. She is multi-talented, too. In addition to English, Jemison speaks fluent Russian, Japanese, and Swahili. She has even appeared on an episode of the TV show "Star Trek: The Next Generation". Jemison founded the International Science Camp in Chicago in 1994, a program designed to stimulate children's interest in science and space.

1-897457-054

Fact or Opinion

A. Check whether each statement below is a fact (F) or an opinion (O).

	F	O

1. Jemison was thrilled when she was called for the space mission.

2. Jemison was the first African-American woman to go into space.

3. Jemison is the youngest child in her family.

4. Jemison enjoyed speaking to people of different cultures.

5. Jemison was a hard-working student in the university.

6. Being a volunteer in a Cambodian refugee camp was never an easy task.

7. Fifteen people were chosen by NASA for astronaut training in 1982.

8. Becoming an astronaut was the greatest achievement of her life.

9. Jemison has no difficulty speaking Russian.

10. It took Jemison ten years to prepare for the space mission.

Your Opinion

B. Answer the questions.

1. Do you want to be an astronaut? Give two reasons.

_____

_____

2. What language(s) can you speak? What other two languages would you like to learn? Why?

_____

_____

ISBN: 978-1-897457-05-4

Participles

- **Participles** *are verb forms that can be used as adjectives.*

   Example: *She is an appointed member of the committee.*

   The word "appointed" is a participle formed from the verb "appoint" describing the noun "member".

C. Change the verbs in parentheses to participles and use them as adjectives in the sentences.

1. Jemison is a (care) _____ person.

2. She is always ready to lend a (help) _____ hand to the needy.

3. The (determine) _____ Jemison was finally selected to fly on Space Shuttle Endeavour.

4. Jemison's (excite) _____ career inspired many Afro-American women.

5. The programs at the International Science Camp are very (stimulate) _____ .

6. The (select) _____ candidates had to undergo months of intensive training.

7. The (challenge) _____ program left many participants (exhaust) _____ .

D. Write your own sentences with the participles as adjectives.

1. changing _____

2. haunted _____

3. encouraging _____

4. disappointed _____

ISBN: 978-1-897457-05-4

Gerunds

- **Gerunds** *are the "ing" form of verbs that serve as nouns.*
  Example: <u>Flying</u> *has always been her dream.*

E. **Change the verbs in parentheses to gerunds and use them as nouns in the sentences.**

1. (sing) _____ is what she enjoys most.

2. (explore) _____ the universe is exciting.

3. Jemison enjoys (help) _____ children learn more about the universe.

4. (give) _____ can be as rewarding as (receive) _____ .

5. (become) _____ an astronaut was what young Jemison wanted.

6. I prefer (swim) _____ to (hike) _____ .

7. Jemison enjoyed (act) _____ in "Star Trek: The Next Generation".

F. **State whether the word in bold in each of the following sentences is a participle or a gerund.**

1. He was noticed because of his **squeaking** shoes. _____

2. **Drinking** lots of water is a good idea on a hot summer day. _____

3. Have you thrown away the **rotten** egg yet? _____

4. **Hiccupping** in the middle of dinner is embarrassing. _____

5. He used a **riding** lawn mower because of the size of the lawn. _____

6. **Riding** a horse is fun but not easy. _____

7. You shouldn't touch the **boiling** water. _____

ISBN: 978-1-897457-05-4

Who Is the Greatest
Hockey Player
of All Time?

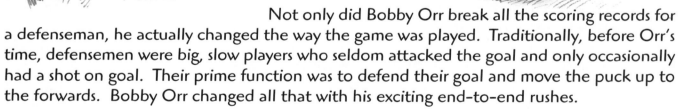

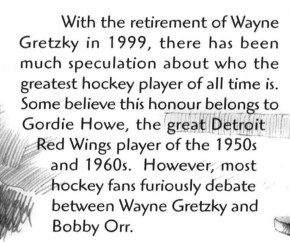

With the retirement of Wayne Gretzky in 1999, there has been much speculation about who the greatest hockey player of all time is. Some believe this honour belongs to Gordie Howe, the great Detroit Red Wings player of the 1950s and 1960s. However, most hockey fans furiously debate between Wayne Gretzky and Bobby Orr.

Not only did Bobby Orr break all the scoring records for a defenseman, he actually changed the way the game was played. Traditionally, before Orr's time, defensemen were big, slow players who seldom attacked the goal and only occasionally had a shot on goal. Their prime function was to defend their goal and move the puck up to the forwards. Bobby Orr changed all that with his exciting end-to-end rushes.

Orr was first spotted by scouts when he was just twelve years old. By the time he reached fifteen, he was distinguishing himself amongst twenty-year-olds in one of the premier Canadian junior leagues. In 1966, his first year in the NHL, he won the Calder Trophy as a rookie of the year. He went on to become the first player ever to win four awards in one season – the MVP, the leading point scorer, the best defenseman, and the play-off MVP. He was also the first defenseman to score 100 points in a season.

Plagued by knee problems, Orr played only 10 regular season games in 1975 but managed to play for Team Canada in 1976, and he was named the tournament MVP. By the 1978 season, Orr had undergone ten knee operations with no successful results, forcing him to retire at the ripe age of thirty. One can only speculate as to what milestones Orr would have reached had he been able to continue to play.

ISBN: 978-1-897457-05-4

Recalling Facts

A. Recall facts from the reading passage and answer each of the following questions in your own words.

1. Besides Orr, name the other two great players that many people regard as the greatest hockey players of all time.

   a. _____   b. _____

2. What made Bobby Orr a different kind of defenseman?

   _____

3. What four awards did Orr win in a single season?

   a. _____   b. _____

   c. _____   d. _____

4. Why did Orr have to quit hockey so early?

   _____

5. What was his personal accomplishment on Team Canada in 1976?

   _____

6. How did Orr change the way the game was played?

   _____

   _____

Your Opinion

B. List the qualities that all great athletes in general possess that set them apart from other players.

a. _____   b. _____   c. _____

d. _____   e. _____   f. _____

ISBN: 978-1-897457-05-4

Verb Tenses

- A **Verb Tense** shows the time of the action of the verb.

- **Present Tense** – action going on in the present
  Example: The boy runs home from school.

- **Past Tense** – action occurred in the past
  Example: The boy ran home.

- **Future Tense** – action will happen in the future; the verb may be accompanied by "shall" or "will"
  Example: The boy will run home.

C. **Fill in the missing verb tenses in the chart below.**

	Present	Past	Future
1.	throw		
2.		won	
3.	begin		
4.		came	
5.	do		
6.			will think
7.	fight		
8.	lose		
9.		wore	
10.	write		
11.		grew	
12.			will shake

ISBN: 978-1-897457-05-4

Forming New Words

D. **Change the word in parentheses to a suitable form to fit the sense of the sentence.**

> **Example:** The boy was (run) _____ to catch the school bus.
> In this case "running" is the suitable form.

1. The puppy was (love) _____ .

2. The (create) _____ person was an artist.

3. She was very (help) _____ to her mother.

4. The boy was told to make himself (use) _____ .

5. The accident was caused by (careless) _____ .

6. He felt (fortune) _____ to have so many friends.

7. The children were (give) _____ gifts at Christmas.

8. They made a (decide) _____ by checking the facts.

9. The tap stopped dripping when the faucet was (tight) _____ .

10. For Math homework, they were asked to do (multiply) _____
    and (divide) _____ .

E. **The following are root words for words from the passage. Write the full words from the passage in the spaces below.**

score	tradition	occasion	belief	distinguish	mile
him	furious	speculate	operate	success	excite

_____   _____   _____

_____   _____   _____

_____   _____   _____

ISBN: 978-1-897457-05-4

The modern bicycle is light, fast, <u>durable</u>, <u>comfortable</u>, and well equipped, such as the models used in the world's most <u>famous</u> bike race – the Tour de France. Original bicycles, however, were very simple mechanical devices.

The first bicycles appeared in the early 19th century. It was a Frenchman from Paris, Pierre Michaux, and his son who built the first bicycle to be mass-marketed. They added pedals to the front wheel of their basic bicycle, thus allowing for <u>propulsion</u>. This design, which was named the "velocipede", resembled the tricycle used by children today. It was a vast improvement over the standard two-wheeler of the time and before long, sales reached 500 units per year – a number considered high by standards of that time.

The next advancement was to make the front wheels larger to improve speed. In 1887 the "safety" bicycle was designed to address <u>safety</u> issues by <u>reducing</u> the size of the front wheel. This model introduced the use of the chain which, when attached by two chainwheels, rotated the back wheel instead of the front. This mechanical principle of volition was based on the ratio between the number of teeth of the front chainwheel to those on the back sprocket. If, for example, the front chainwheel had 32 teeth and the rear sprocket 8, then the ratio would be 32:8; this meant that for every rotation of the front cogwheel, there were four <u>rotations</u> of the rear one, a ratio of 4 to 1. Consequently, the bicycle could have wheels of equal measure and actually increase speed.

One of the most important advancements of the safety bicycle was the addition of gears. This allowed for the use of <u>different</u> gears for particular situations. A "derailer" would shift the chain from one sprocket to another creating a new pairing of chainwheels with different ratios of teeth, and therefore, various <u>levels</u> of pedaling difficulty.

As a result of pollution and environmental concerns, there has been <u>renewed</u> interest in biking in cities worldwide.

Bicycles— Then and Now

ISBN: 978-1-897457-05-4

Matching Details

A. Match the facts by drawing lines from Column A to Column B.

Column A

1. safety bicycle

2. modern bicycle

3. Tour de France

4. velocipede

5. 1887

6. 32 teeth

7. 8 teeth

8. 4 to 1

9. environmental concerns

10. derailer

Column B

A. resembled a tricycle

B. safety bicycle was designed

C. ratio of gears

D. reason for today's use

E. shifts the chain

F. international race

G. front chainwheel

H. smaller front wheel

I. fast, durable, comfortable

J. rear chainwheel

Your Opinion

B. What do you think are the reasons for the renewed interest in cycling today?

_____

_____

ISBN: 978-1-897457-05-4

Subject and Verb Agreement

- The **Verb** in a sentence must agree with its subject and must change to the tense needed in the sentence.

   Example 1: We go. He goes. She goes. They go.
   Note the changes in the verb "go".

   Example 2: He is ... / She is ... / We are ... / They are ... / You are ...
   These are forms of the infinitive "to be".

C.   Circle the correct noun or verb for each of the sentences below.

1. The first day of the school year is, were an exciting day.

2. We, She is the new student in the school.

3. The teacher tell, told the students about all the rules.

4. When the recess bell rang, ring , the students went, goes outside.

5. Paul and John was, were the first students to get to the schoolyard.

6. The children always play, plays basketball for the entire recess.

7. When the bell rings, rung , they will came, come inside.

8. The students was, were seated in rows.

9. One of the teachers could speak, spoke three languages.

10. After school, activities was, were offered to the students.

11. Some chooses, chose sports. Others preferred, prefers clubs.

12. The school bus take, took some of the students home at the end of the day.

ISBN: 978-1-897457-05-4

Synonyms and Antonyms

- **Synonyms** are words with similar meanings. **Antonyms** are words with opposite meanings.

D. Read the clues and complete the words. They are the underlined words in the passage.

1. well-known   __ A __ __ U __   (Synonym)

2. stages   __ __ V __ L __   (Synonym)

3. enlarging   __ E __ __ C __ N __   (Antonym)

4. turns   __ O __ A __ I __ __ __   (Synonym)

5. forward motion   __ R __ P __ __ __ __ O __   (Synonym)

6. danger   __ A __ __ T __   (Antonym)

7. old   __ E __ E __ E __   (Antonym)

8. weak   __ __ R __ __ L __   (Antonym)

9. similar   __ I __ F __ R __ __ __   (Antonym)

10. cozy   __ __ M __ O __ T __ __ L __   (Synonym)

ISBN: 978-1-897457-05-4

On September 9, 1954, 100,000 enthusiastic people waited by the shore of Lake Ontario at the Canadian National Exhibition (CNE). They were there to greet a relatively unknown 16-year-old girl, Marilyn Bell, whom they hoped to see emerge from the water after her swim across Lake Ontario. By approximately 8:00 p.m., a tiny speck appeared on the water close to the shore. The crowd cheered wildly, for Miss Bell was about to do what no man or woman had accomplished before – conquer Lake Ontario.

It took Marilyn 21 hours of continuous swimming in the chilly, sometimes rough, Lake Ontario waters. Overnight she had become Canada's most famous female athlete since the great figure skater, Barbara Ann Scott. Bell's historic quest captured the hearts and minds of Canadians across the country.

Marathon swimming is a sport of personal challenge where an athlete pits himself or herself against insurmountable odds. Although very young, Marilyn was not an inexperienced

Marilyn Bell –
Marathon Swimmer
(1)

long distance swimmer. She had been a member of the Lakeshore Swimming Club and had trained under the well-known swim coach, Gus Ryder. Marilyn had competed in many races, and just eight weeks before the Lake Ontario swim, she swam the Atlantic City marathon, a gruelling 20-mile race in the ocean. She spent a total of 10 hours in the water and finished two hours ahead of the nearest female competitor and came seventh overall out of forty swimmers.

This Lake Ontario marathon crossing was sponsored by the CNE. However, Marilyn was not officially invited to take part. The CNE had invited American swimmer, Florence Chadwick, to attempt the crossing and offered her a $10,000 prize upon completion. Marilyn was joined by Winnie Leuszler as unpaid and uninvited participants.

ISBN: 978-1-897457-05-4

Fact or Opinion

Facts are based on the exact information from the passage. Opinion is your personal view based on the facts from the reading passage.

A. Place "F" for fact or "O" for opinion beside each statement.

1. _____ The spectators went wild when Bell arrived at the CNE.

2. _____ It took Bell 21 hours to cross Lake Ontario.

3. _____ Marathon swimming is about personal challenge.

4. _____ The CNE sponsored the marathon swim.

5. _____ Florence Chadwick was offered a lot of money to participate.

6. _____ Bell was not invited to swim.

7. _____ Swimming in the lake was not a pleasant experience.

8. _____ Bell became one of Canada's greatest female athletes.

9. _____ Marilyn was not new to marathon swimming.

10. _____ Lake Ontario can be treacherous.

11. _____ Bell did fairly well in the Atlantic City marathon.

12. _____ 100,000 people came to cheer her on.

Your Opinion

B. Give your opinion to the following questions.

1. Why was Marilyn Bell's marathon swim considered such a heroic event?

    _____

    _____

    _____

2. Do you think it was fair that Marilyn Bell was not invited to swim and not offered any money?

    _____

    _____

    _____

ISBN: 978-1-897457-05-4

Combining Sentences

- **Short Sentences** *can sometimes be effective. However, more often it is useful to combine short sentences. There are two easy ways to combine sentences:*
    1. *use a conjunction such as "and", "or", or "but";*
    2. *make one of the short sentences a dependent sentence by connecting it with a subordinate conjunction.*

C.   Combine the following short sentences.

1.   Winter in Canada can be cold. Some areas of the country are colder than others.

   _____

2.   They played basketball. They played on the same team.

   _____

3.   The choir sang. The choir sang at the ceremony. The ceremony was graduation.

   _____

4.   The animals were in the zoo. The animals were caged. The animals were wild.

   _____

5.   It was a hot day. They went swimming. They swam in the public pool nearby.

   _____

D.   From the basic sentences below, develop descriptive, detailed sentences.

1.   The _____ game was played in _____ after

   _____ .

2.   The _____ man walked _____ across the

   _____ to _____ .

3.   Although _____ , the students gathered in

   _____ to _____ .

4.   The _____ wind blew _____ across the

   _____ while the children _____ .

ISBN: 978-1-897457-05-4

Writing Descriptions

E. The topics below are related to the passage "Marilyn Bell – Marathon Swimmer (1)". Create one or two descriptive sentences for each topic.

> *Use any or all of the descriptive words provided with each topic to add detail to your sentences. Change these words to suit the use in your sentences.*

1. The waters of Lake Ontario

   choppy chilly rough battling vast waves dark struggling

   _____

   _____

   _____

2. The crowd of people waiting at the CNE

   anxious expectant cheering surprised excited clapping

   _____

   _____

   _____

3. Marilyn Bell emerges from Lake Ontario

   chilled exhausted staggering jubilant ecstatic proudly

   _____

   _____

   _____

ISBN: 978-1-897457-05-4

Marilyn knew that she was an unwelcome participant in the Lake Ontario challenge swim. She felt that since it was a Canadian sponsored event, a Canadian swimmer should take part. Marilyn later confessed that she was not sure that she could make it herself, but she was also unsure that Chadwick could make it. On September 8, 1954, the swimmers stepped into the chilly, 21°C Lake Ontario water at Youngstown, New York. Bell was swimming for Canada and the much-anticipated race was on!

It didn't take long for Marilyn to show her strength. Five kilometres from the American shore, she had overtaken Chadwick, and by 6:00 a.m., Chadwick had been pulled from the water after 26 km. Leuszler quit at the 32 km mark, leaving Bell as the only competitor.

The swimming conditions were less than ideal. It rained through the night and the water temperature dropped to 16°C. The water was choppy but Bell managed to maintain a steady 60 strokes a minute, for a two-mile-an-hour pace. Her biggest difficulty was boredom. On more than one occasion, Marilyn fell asleep and her coach, Gus Ryder, had to wake her up. She was fed baby food and syrup on a stick alongside the boat.

Marilyn Bell – Marathon Swimmer (2)

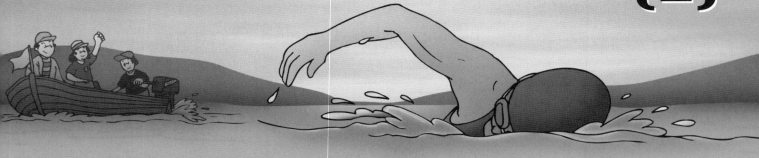

On the Canadian side, the radio stations had been broadcasting her progress and thousands of extra newspapers were being printed to meet the public demand for this incredible story. When she completed the 51.5 km swim and sat in an ambulance recovering, she exclaimed that she felt terrific. The CNE gave Bell the prize money and she received another $50,000 worth of gifts. She became an instant celebrity and a national treasure.

Marilyn Bell went on to conquer the English Channel the following year and attempted the treacherous Straits of Juan de Fuca. She failed to complete the Juan de Fuca swim but two weeks later, she covered her skin with Vaseline to offset the cold, and successfully completed the swim.

Marilyn Bell retired from marathon swimming at the age of eighteen, much to the disappointment of her fans.

ISBN: 978-1-897457-05-4

Recalling Information

A. Write "T" for true statements and "F" for false ones in the spaces provided.

1. _____ Marilyn was swimming for Canada.

2. _____ Lake Ontario was a warm 32°C the day of the swim.

3. _____ Bell's pace was 60 strokes per minute.

4. _____ Bell passed Chadwick after only 5 km into the swim.

5. _____ The race began at the CNE.

6. _____ Bell received no money but only prizes for her effort.

7. _____ Bell never swam again after her Lake Ontario victory.

8. _____ Bell fell asleep during her race.

9. _____ Bell ate syrup from a stick.

10. _____ Chadwick finished the race in second place.

11. _____ Swimming Lake Ontario was boring for Bell.

12. _____ The distance across the lake was 51.5 km.

Your Opinion

B. Answer the questions with your own opinion.

1. Why do you think Marilyn Bell retired from swimming at the age of eighteen when her best years were still ahead?

_____

_____

2. How did Gus Ryder, her coach, help her by being alongside her throughout the swim?

_____

_____

ISBN: 978-1-897457-05-4

Prepositions and Phrases

- A **Preposition** shows the connection of a noun or pronoun to other words in a sentence.

  Some common prepositions are: in, under, around, between, among, for, at, over, with, behind, into, and of.

- A **Phrase** can be adjective or adverb in nature. That is, it can describe a noun or the action of a verb. When it describes the action of a verb, it often answers the questions where or when.

  Example : The girls of St. Peter's School sang a song in the auditorium.

  Note the prepositions "of" and "in". Each of them introduces a phrase.

  The phrase "of St. Peter's School" tells which girls they were. Since "girls" is a noun, subject of the sentence, then "of St. Peter's School" must be an adjective phrase.

  The phrase "in the auditorium" tells where the singing (verb) was done. Therefore it is an adverb phrase.

C. **Place Adj. (adjective) or Adv. (adverb) in the space provided to identify the phrases underlined.**

1. <u>In the morning</u>, he walked to school alone. _____

2. <u>At night</u>, the house was scary. _____

3. The "Bells <u>of St. Mary's</u>" is a favourite Christmas movie. _____

4. The children <u>in the daycare</u> were asleep on their cots. _____

5. He was told to place his books <u>in his desk</u>. _____

6. <u>At sunrise</u>, they will go fishing. _____

7. He hid under the bed <u>in his brother's bedroom</u>. _____

8. The treats were divided <u>among the classmates</u>. _____

9. He played hockey at the arena <u>in the recreation centre</u>. _____

10. <u>On the coffee table</u> sat a vase of flowers and some photos. _____

ISBN: 978-1-897457-05-4

Composing an Interview

D. Write the questions that you will ask Ms. Bell about her heroic swim.

> *Pretend you are a newspaper reporter and have been granted an exclusive interview. Use the facts you have learned from the passages (parts 1 and 2) to help make up your questions.*

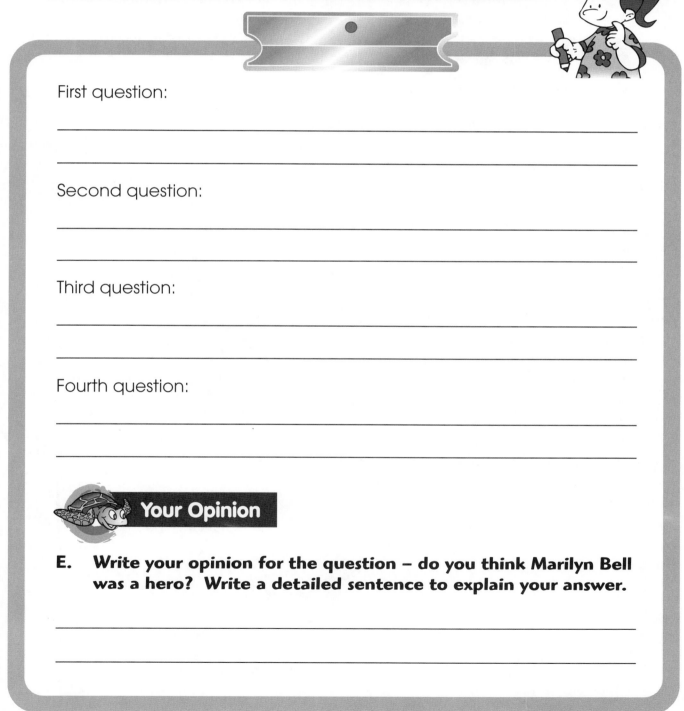

First question:

_____

_____

Second question:

_____

_____

Third question:

_____

_____

Fourth question:

_____

_____

Your Opinion

E. Write your opinion for the question – do you think Marilyn Bell was a hero? Write a detailed sentence to explain your answer.

_____

_____

ISBN: 978-1-897457-05-4

Plants are bright colourful adornments of nature that feed on sunlight and water. Or so we think. Many plants are, in fact, carnivorous. Science fiction movies have frightened us with horror stories of man-eating plants that swallow human beings whole. This notion may seem absurd to us, but it is an ugly truth for many an unsuspecting insect.

Meat-Eating Plants

Some species of plants require the meat of an insect as a dietary supplement. There are two types of meat-eating plants. Some plants such as the Venus Flytrap actually move to capture their prey. Other plants sit and wait and let the insects trap themselves. The Sticky Sundew is covered with sticky hairs that produce a type of glue that sticks to the unsuspecting insect when it lands. The hairs then close over it and it is absorbed into the plant. The Cobra Lily, named for its snake-like appearance, lures insects with its nectar. Once an insect enters the plant, it becomes confused by the light shining through the leaves. Following this light to escape, it becomes exhausted and drops into the liquid of the plant.

The best known predator plant is the Venus Flytrap. Insects are attracted by the unusual leaf tips and cannot resist landing on them. Adding to this lure is the promise of food from sweet smelling nectar. After the insect alights on the surface of the leaf, two kidney-shaped lobes, triggered by sensitive bristles at the top of the leaf, snap shut. After about half an hour, the Venus Flytrap will secrete enzymes and acids which will slowly digest the insect. Full digestion of an insect may take up to two weeks and the trap will then be prepared for another victim. When the Venus Flytrap is ready to eat again, the trap opens and the exoskeleton of the devoured insect is blown away in the wind.

ISBN: 978-1-897457-05-4

Remembering Details

A. Fill in the blanks with the appropriate words from the list provided.

> Venus Flytrap   enzymes   diet   carnivorous   wind   insects
> nectar   Sticky Sundew   weeks   confused   exoskeleton

Some plants are 1._____ , that is they eat meat. They feed on unsuspecting 2._____ . For some plants, meat is a necessary supplement to their regular 3._____ . The 4._____ actually moves to catch its prey while the 5._____ has a sticky surface that traps its catch. The Cobra Lily lures insects with its sweet smelling 6._____ . Once an insect enters the Cobra Lily, it becomes 7._____ by the light and loses its way, eventually drowning in the plant's juice. The Venus Flytrap breaks down and digests an insect using 8._____ and acids. Full digestion of an insect can take up to two 9._____ . The Venus Flytrap, after digesting its victim, lets the 10._____ blow away the discarded 11._____ of the insect. Once this is done, the leaves open up again ready for the next meal.

In Your Own Words

B. Suggest three titles for horror movies about killer plants.

(Be humorous if you choose.)

1. _____

2. _____

3. _____

ISBN: 978-1-897457-05-4

Subordinate Clauses

- A **Subordinate Clause** has a noun and a verb and usually begins with a connecting word or conjunction. Unlike a sentence, it cannot stand on its own without more information to complete its meaning.

  Examples: 1. although I enjoy eating pizza

  2. when I was walking home from school

- These subordinate clauses cannot stand on their own as sentences. They require more information to convey a complete thought as written below:

  Examples: 1. I want to have Indian food although I enjoy eating pizza.

  2. When I was walking home from school, I met Kate.

C. **Place parentheses ( ) around the subordinate clause in each of the following sentences.**

1. Whenever I run too fast, my legs ache.

2. After we played the game, we ordered pizza.

3. The police arrived quickly because it was an emergency.

4. He knew he could stay as long as he wanted.

5. Even if they had tried harder, they could not have won the game.

6. She rode off on her bike as the sun set.

7. He acted as if no one could see what he was doing.

8. Although the students were well-behaved, they stayed in for recess.

9. She watched television while she waited for her friend to call.

10. Mr. Wilman rushed back to his office as soon as he got the message.

11. We were all happy even though we were not the champions.

12. I don't know what happened since I wasn't there.

13. The UFO disappeared before I could take a photo of it.

ISBN: 978-1-897457-05-4

Searching for Synonyms

D. **Find and circle the synonyms for the words in the list. The synonyms are words in the passage.**

addition

lands

leak

victim

dazed

food

decorations

hunter

strange

eaten

b	o	w	p	r	e	d	a	t	o	r	d
e	k	o	l	t	z	r	m	s	b	y	i
k	c	c	p	s	f	a	x	w	j	u	e
r	o	s	u	p	p	l	e	m	e	n	t
u	n	h	g	r	p	i	q	e	j	u	a
l	f	n	c	e	a	g	r	h	e	s	r
x	u	n	s	y	d	h	u	c	v	u	y
p	s	e	c	r	e	t	e	a	g	a	p
j	e	n	t	w	e	s	b	u	e	l	u
a	d	o	r	n	m	e	n	t	s	q	s
n	g	d	e	v	o	u	r	e	d	m	k
w	c	r	a	f	t	i	v	y	o	r	e

Writing Sentences

E. **Make a sentence with each group of words from the passage.**

1. predator prey devoured

_____

_____

2. dietary supplement unusual

_____

_____

ISBN: 978-1-897457-05-4

With the discovery of the new world, more specifically the Caribbean, by the famous explorer Christopher Columbus, trade began between North America and Europe. Although this trade was <u>profitable</u> and great wealth lay in the transport of goods from the Caribbean, it was not without problems. Rough seas were always a concern, but a greater problem was the potential attack by pirates.

The trade <u>routes</u> across the Atlantic were well-known to pirates, some of whom had been employed as sailors on trading vessels. A pirate ship, equipped with cannons and ruthless men, would pull up alongside a trading vessel, jump aboard, and take control. If the trading ship's captain or crew resisted, they would be killed. The pirates would take the goods and recruit new members to piracy from the trading vessel's <u>crew</u>. Not all pirates were kind enough to let their victims live. Some murdered the crew of the ships and left the vessels covered with dead bodies to float on the seas, serving as a message to other ships not to resist takeover if approached.

Many sailors were attracted to the <u>carefree</u> life of a pirate travelling the high seas and getting rich from the gold and jewels found on the trading vessels. After a few successful <u>raids</u>, they could <u>retire</u> to one of the <u>exotic</u> Caribbean islands or head home to their <u>native</u> land.

Not all pirates were bandits. There was a distinct group called privateers who were actually hired by a country to pirate the trading vessels of a rival country. The British, for example, hired privateers to attack Spanish vessels. They required only 10% of the <u>booty</u> obtained from the pirated <u>vessel</u>. When England took Jamaica from the Spanish, they hired Captain Henry Morgan (the well-known face on rum bottles sold today) to protect the island by attacking Spanish ships. Morgan became wealthy from the "booty" he obtained and received favourable recognition by the English navy.

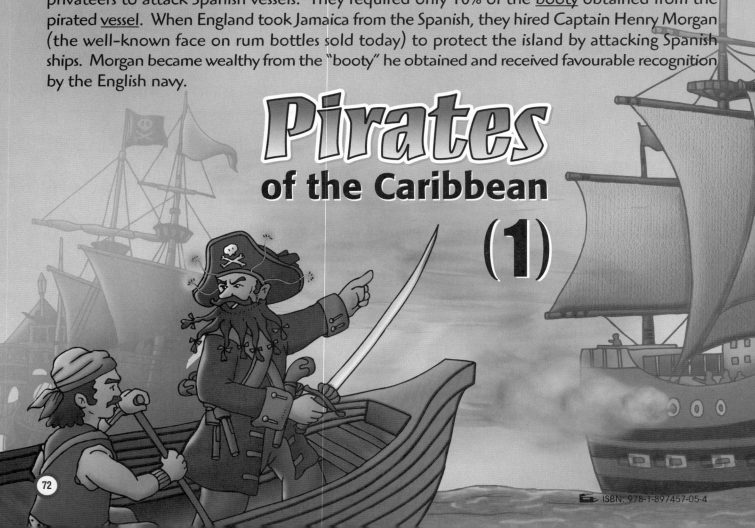

Pirates
of the Caribbean
(1)

ISBN: 978-1-897457-05-4

Cause and Effect

A. **Place a check mark beside the correct "cause" listed for each "effect" stated.**

1. Pirates were anxious to attack trading ships.

   A. _____ The pirates wanted revenge.

   B. _____ The ships were carrying valuable goods.

   C. _____ The pirates were at war.

2. Pirates were familiar with the trading routes.

   A. _____ The pirates had been sailors on trading ships.

   B. _____ Pirates had stolen the trading route maps.

   C. _____ The pirates were born in the Caribbean.

3. Pirates sometimes killed their victims unnecessarily.

   A. _____ The pirates panicked when they were robbing a ship.

   B. _____ Dead sailors warned other trading ships not to resist.

   C. _____ Pirates did not take prisoners.

4. Many sailors wanted to be pirates.

   A. _____ Pirates were able to travel.

   B. _____ Pirates lived a carefree life.

   C. _____ Sailing was hard work.

5. Not all pirates were criminals.

   A. _____ Privateers were hired by various countries.

   B. _____ Some pirates gave away all the goods they stole.

   C. _____ Some pirates were kind and friendly.

6. Henry Morgan was a famous pirate.

   A. _____ He killed many sailors.

   B. _____ He was hired by England to protect Jamaica.

   C. _____ He liked to drink rum.

ISBN: 978-1-897457-05-4

Building Sentences with Phrases and Clauses

- **Phrases and Clauses** can be added to a sentence to make it more interesting.

    Example: The players on _____ were excited because _____ .

    The word "on" is a preposition used to introduce a phrase and the word "because" is a subordinate conjunction used to introduce a clause.

    You might have added the following phrase and clause to the sample sentence above: The players on <u>the winning team</u> were excited because <u>they won the championship</u>.

Be creative!

B.   Make up new sentences by adding your own phrases and clauses to the sentences below.

1.   Whenever _____ , she is happy.

2.   The key in _____ was stuck

     because _____ .

3.   The horses of _____ stopped

     running when _____ .

4.   The gift in _____ was hidden

     until _____ .

5.   Because _____ , he had to go to

     sleep in _____ .

6.   He sat in _____ and waited while

     _____ .

7.   Before _____ , he was the best

     hockey player on _____ .

ISBN: 978-1-897457-05-4

Crossword Puzzle

C. Read the clues and complete the crossword puzzle with the underlined words from the passage.

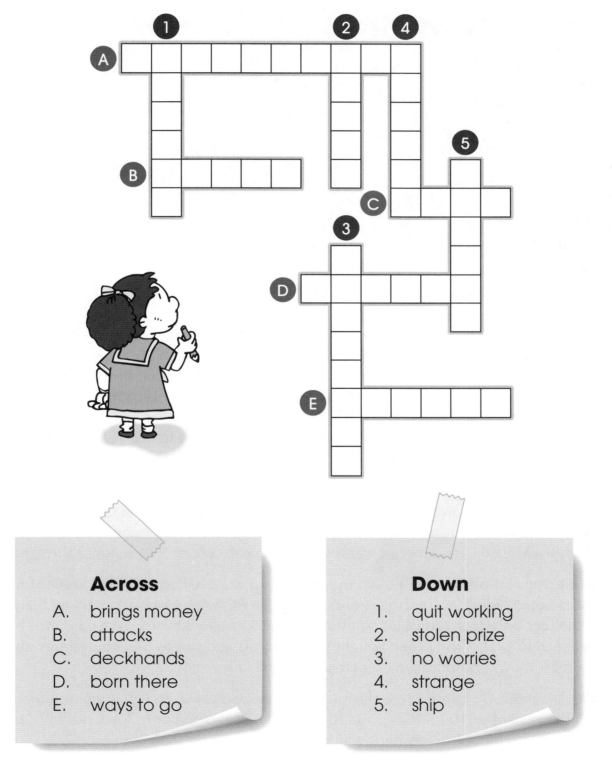

Across

A. brings money
B. attacks
C. deckhands
D. born there
E. ways to go

Down

1. quit working
2. stolen prize
3. no worries
4. strange
5. ship

ISBN: 978-1-897457-05-4

Pirates
of the Caribbean (2)

Pirates, such as Captain Henry Morgan, were also referred to as buccaneers. They became legendary as stories about their ruthlessness and their skills at pirating spread throughout the Caribbean and the southern coast of North America. The most notorious pirate of them all was Edward Teach, better known as Blackbeard. He was tall and muscular with a long beard braided with bright ribbons that hung down to his chest. He was a fearful sight. When he went into battle, he would put slow burning fuses in his hair, creating a smoky haze that surrounded his head. If his opponents put up a fight, he would teach them a lesson. In one case, he cut off the nose of a Portuguese sailor; in another, he killed one of his own men just to remind his crew of how evil he was. It was acts like these that spread his reputation far and wide and made piracy easy for him.

Piracy was taking its toll on the economy of the major trading countries. Doing business in the Caribbean and the Carolina coast was becoming very expensive. The Governor of Virginia, Alexander Spotswood, put up a reward of 100 British pounds (approximately $230) for the capture of Blackbeard. This amount was roughly ten years' wages for a sailor at the time.

A British naval officer named Maynard took up the challenge with a crew of 60, and found Blackbeard hiding in a North Carolina inlet. The next day, Maynard attacked Blackbeard and on the second attack found himself face to face with Blackbeard. Maynard shot him but Blackbeard didn't fall. They then fought with swords, and just as Blackbeard was about to deliver a fatal blow, one of Maynard's crew shot and killed him.

With Blackbeard's death came the end of piracy. However, the governor refused to give Maynard the reward of 100 British pounds. Instead he gave him only 3 pounds ($7) and half that to his crew. This paltry payment was hardly worth risking their lives.

ISBN: 978-1-897457-05-4

Understanding Content

A. For each statement below, write the exact sentence or phrase from the story that supports that statement.

1. Pirates became legends for the awful things that they did.

    _____

2. The pirates were hurting the economy of trading countries because of their thieving.

    _____

3. Edward Teach was unforgettable because of his appearance.

    _____

4. Teach sometimes performed acts of incredible cruelty.

    _____

5. Piracy was easy for Blackbeard because of his reputation.

    _____

6. Maynard, an English naval officer, went looking for Blackbeard.

    _____

7. Maynard was lucky Blackbeard didn't kill him.

    _____

8. Maynard's efforts were for nothing.

    _____

9. The death of Blackbeard changed everything.

    _____

10. It was not worth it to try to capture Blackbeard.

    _____

ISBN: 978-1-897457-05-4

Rules of Capitalization

1. Capitalize the first word in a sentence.
2. Capitalize all proper nouns that name individuals, places, and organizations, but not "the" or "of".
3. Capitalize titles when they come before a person's name.
4. Capitalize all government titles, but not "the" or "of".
5. Capitalize the first word of a quotation.
6. Capitalize points on the compass only when they are used as a distinct part of the country, i.e. the North, but not "he went North".

B.   Capitalize the words that should be capitalized.

Write directly on top of the letters you are changing. The number after each sentence tells you the number of capital letters in that sentence.

1.   the injured man called for dr. smith to come to his aid. (3)

2.   the earl of sandwich became famous for his invention of the sandwich. (3)

3.   the mona lisa is one of da vinci's most famous paintings. (4)

4.   lisa moore attended the university of toronto and received a degree in english. (5)

5.   she asked, "what time will professor higgins give his speech about pioneers of the wild west?" (7)

6.   the japanese family arrived in new york on american airlines and stayed at the hilton hotel in upper manhattan. (9)

ISBN: 978-1-897457-05-4

Writing Poetry

- **Poems** often have strict rhyming schemes. Here are two sample rhyming schemes:

Example 1 – scheme   a b a b

The sun was bright	a
The wind was low	b
The bird took flight	a
His wings aglow	b

Example 2 – scheme   a a b b

Swinging on a tree	a
She felt happy and free	a
Gliding up into the air	b
Without a single care	b

In example one, the first and third lines rhyme as do the second and fourth. In example two, the first and second lines rhyme as do the third and fourth.

- The lines grouped together with a rhyming scheme form a stanza.

C. **Create a poem of one stanza about Pirates of the Caribbean using either of the rhyming schemes above.**

Rhyming Words

limb - trim	teach - reach
raid - afraid	death - breath
battle - rattle	beard - feared
mate - fate	aboard - sword
booty - snooty	glorious - notorious
mess - confess	coast - boast - most
fight - might - sight	

Here are some rhyming words to help you get started. If you prefer, create your own rhyming words.

Title: _____

_____

_____

_____

_____

ISBN: 978-1-897457-05-4

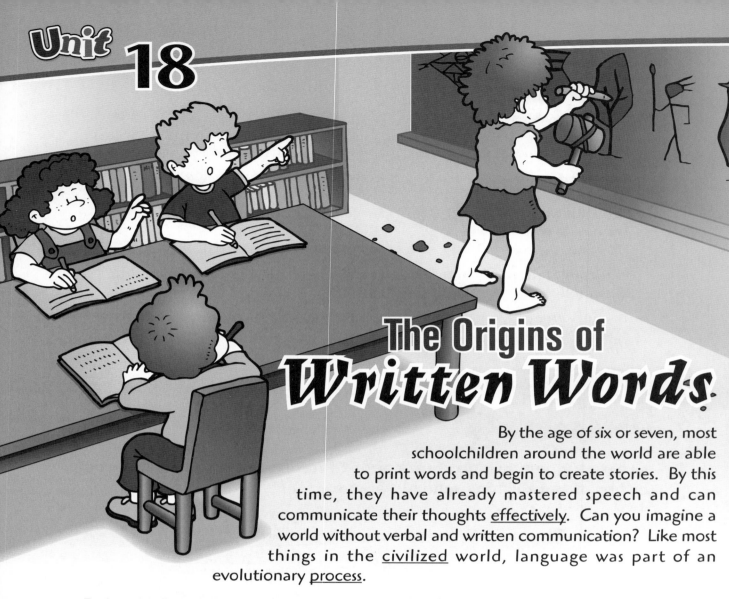

The Origins of Written Words

By the age of six or seven, most schoolchildren around the world are able to print words and begin to create stories. By this time, they have already mastered speech and can communicate their thoughts <u>effectively</u>. Can you imagine a world without verbal and written communication? Like most things in the <u>civilized</u> world, language was part of an evolutionary <u>process</u>.

Early man, known as Homo sapiens, communicated by drawing pictures on the walls of caves. They would draw pictures of their hunts for food and of important <u>social</u> and personal family events. It was not until 3000 BCE that actual writing, a method of recording language sounds, came into being. Early forms of writing were traced back to the Sumerians of Mesopotamia. Their writing was made up of <u>symbols</u> called logograms that stood for words or phrases. This <u>system</u> <u>evolved</u> to include representations of syllables. Thus the Sumerians were using both logograms and syllabic forms to <u>create</u> writing.

To avoid <u>confusion</u>, sounds, such as the vowel and consonant sounds that we use today, were given <u>specific</u> symbols. This was the early creation of an alphabetic system. There are not many symbols needed to create a language. For example, the English language uses an alphabet with only 26 letters but there are over 500,000 English words listed in the Oxford Dictionary.

The Egyptians developed hieroglyphics, a system of writing, approximately a hundred years after the Sumerian system. Many forms of writing were adapted by other peoples until about the year 1500 BCE when a partially alphabetic system was created. This marked the early stages of writing as we know it today. The Greeks are credited with separating vowel and consonant sounds by 750 BCE, thereby creating the fully alphabetic system, which paved the way for the full development of organized language.

ISBN: 978-1-897457-05-4

 **The Main Idea**

A. **Below are summary ideas for each paragraph. Place a check mark in the space provided for the summary statement that best suits each paragraph.**

Paragraph One

A. ____ Language has evolved over the years.

B. ____ Children have learned how to write.

C. ____ What if the world had no communication

Paragraph Two

A. ____ Early writing was in the form of drawing.

B. ____ The roots of early language

C. ____ Homo sapiens – early man

Paragraph Three

A. ____ Sounds were given symbols.

B. ____ The alphabet was created.

C. ____ A dictionary was written.

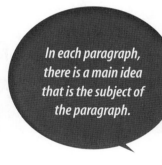

In each paragraph, there is a main idea that is the subject of the paragraph.

Paragraph Four

A. ____ The origins of the alphabet system for writing

B. ____ The Greeks separated vowels and consonants.

C. ____ Egyptians developed hieroglyphics.

B. **Place a number from 1 – 5 beside each of the events to indicate the order in which they occurred.**

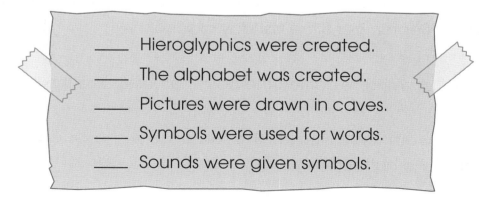

____ Hieroglyphics were created.

____ The alphabet was created.

____ Pictures were drawn in caves.

____ Symbols were used for words.

____ Sounds were given symbols.

ISBN: 978-1-897457-05-4

Using the Comma

1. Use a comma to separate words in a series or list.
   Example: We played hockey, baseball, basketball, and tennis.

2. Use a comma between adjectives describing a noun.
   Example: The tall, thin, poorly dressed man walked by.

3. Use a comma to separate a noun in apposition.
   Example: My friend, Paul, came to visit me.

4. Use a comma in dates.
   Example: Her birthday was July 22, 1953.

5. Use a comma after long subordinate clauses that appear first.
   Example: After we ate the meal that mother prepared, we went for a walk.

6. Use a comma to set off a direct quotation.
   Example: She asked, "May I use your telephone?"

C. Punctuate the sentences below.

The number at the end of each sentence represents the number of punctuation marks needed.

1. Where would one go to find good weather interesting shopping friendly people and inexpensive accommodations (4)

2. Why do certain sports such as hockey golf and tennis cost so much to play (3)

3. Hand in your test papers your special pencils and your question sheets now (3)

4. "Get out of bed right now or you'll be late for school" my mother yelled "Don't you realize it's September 5 the first day of school" (4)

5. John's father Mr. Williams carried the balls the bases and the bats (5)

6. When Susan went shopping at the local store she bought milk bread cheese eggs and butter (6)

ISBN: 978-1-897457-05-4

Word Building Chart

D. Fill in the chart below to create new words from the "original" words taken from the passage.

Locate each word in the passage and learn its meaning from the sentence in which it appears.

Original Word (from passage)	New Word (add prefix/suffix)	Meaning
1. effectively		
2. civilized		
3. process		
4. social		
5. symbols		
6. system		
7. evolved		
8. create		
9. confusion		
10. specific		

ISBN: 978-1-897457-05-4

Recalling Details

A. **Place a check mark beside the best answer to complete each statement.**

1. One of Bobby Orr's accomplishments was that

   A. _____ he was better than Wayne Gretsky.

   B. _____ he was the first player to win four awards in one season.

   C. _____ he played for Team Canada.

2. Orr retired early because

   A. _____ he wanted to start a business.

   B. _____ he was too old to play any longer.

   C. _____ his knee was too damaged.

3. The most famous bike race in the world is

   A. _____ the Tour de France.

   B. _____ the American Cross Country Race.

   C. _____ the Ride Across Europe.

4. The most important development of the safety bicycle was

   A. _____ creating a larger front wheel.

   B. _____ the addition of gears.

   C. _____ creating a smaller front wheel.

5. Mae Jemison got her degree in chemical engineering from

   A. _____ Oxford University.

   B. _____ University of Toronto.

   C. _____ Stanford University.

6. Just eight weeks before the Lake Ontario swim, Bell swam the

   A. _____ Pacific Ocean Marathon.

   B. _____ English Channel.

   C. _____ Atlantic City Marathon.

ISBN: 978-1-897457-05-4

7. Marilyn Bell swam across Lake Ontario from

   A. _____ Youngstown to Toronto.

   B. _____ Toronto to Youngstown.

   C. _____ Buffalo to Toronto.

8. Bell's reward for her heroic effort was

   A. _____ $50,000 in prizes.

   B. _____ $10,000 award from the CNE.

   C. _____ $50,000 in gifts and $10,000 from CNE.

9. Meat-eating plants like to devour

   A. _____ small animals.

   B. _____ human beings.

   C. _____ insects.

10. Sailors were easily recruited as pirates because they

   A. _____ enjoyed stealing and torturing people.

   B. _____ liked the idea of travelling the high seas and getting rich.

   C. _____ wanted to stop vessels from trading with other countries.

11. Not all pirates were actual bandits. Some were

   A. _____ hired by some countries to attack the vessels of rival countries.

   B. _____ secret agents out to capture other pirates.

   C. _____ lost at sea.

12. Blackbeard was the most feared pirate because

   A. _____ he was small but fearless.

   B. _____ he was cunning and hard to catch.

   C. _____ he performed acts of cruelty as a warning to sailors.

13. The earliest form of written communication was

   A. _____ hieroglyphics.

   B. _____ cave drawings.

   C. _____ alphabetic system.

ISBN: 978-1-897457-05-4

Tenses and Verb Agreement

B. Choose the proper word to match the sense and tense of each sentence.

1. Dad and I will go, went _____ fishing this Saturday.

2. The team wins, won _____ the hockey game last night.

3. Susan and Debbie tells, told _____ the small children a story.

4. The boys was, were _____ waiting for the girls to finish, finished

    _____ using the baseball diamond.

5. When the bus come, came , _____ the students line, lined

    _____ up to take, took _____ a seat.

6. The teacher was, were _____ pleased with the behaviour of the

    students who went, go _____ on the school trip.

Participles and Gerunds

C. Fill in the blanks with the participles or gerunds of the given words.

1. He was noticed because of his (squeak) _____ shoes.

2. Have you thrown away the (rot) _____ eggs?

3. The (confuse) _____ road signs are driving me crazy.

4. Eric was an (uninvite) _____ guest to the party.

5. I think (tell) _____ the truth is what we should do.

6. (talk) _____ on a cell phone in a meeting is inconsiderate.

7. The neighbours were helping Janet find her (lose) _____ puppy.

ISBN: 978-1-897457-05-4

Prepositions and Phrases

D. Complete the adjective and adverb phrases for the following sentences.

1. The players on _____ arrived at _____ for
    their _____ against _____ .

2. In _____ Grandma found her old photo album from
    _____ .

3. At _____ it was time to get on _____ and
    head home for _____ .

4. In _____ he woke up and pulled his clothes from
    _____ and put his books in _____ .

Building Sentences with Subordinate Clauses

E. Complete the following sentences.

1. When the students hear the recess bell, _____
    _____

2. After they ate their lunch, _____
    _____

3. Although his uncle was angry, _____
    _____

4. Since the children missed the game, _____
    _____

87

ISBN: 978-1-897457-05-4

Punctuation and Capitalization

Recall the rules of capitalization given in Unit 17 and the examples of sentence punctuation given in Unit 18.

F.   Punctuate each of the sentences below.

1.   is it cold outside she asked

2.   sams birthday was august 15 1989

3.   stop don't move shouted the police officer

4.   dr smith worked for the canadian ministry of health

5.   the small frightened siamese cat curled up in her lap

6.   on a recent trip to toronto his family went to watch the blue jays

Building Vocabulary

G.   Make changes to the words in parentheses to suit the sentences. Be careful of verb tense, subject–verb agreement, and parts of speech.

Example: John (fly) _____ in a small airplane last week.

You would change "fly" to "flew" to suit the verb tense.

1.   He was (run) _____ when he tripped and fell.

2.   The sun (rise) _____ in the east and (set) _____ in the west every day.

3.   He was (satisfy) _____ to have finished second in the race.

4.   The school work was not (complete) _____ on time.

5.   The company slogan read, "Satisfaction (guarantee) _____ ."

6.   The (replace) _____ top on the bottle was convenient.

7.   He couldn't tell the (different) _____ between the twins.

8.   He ran (swift) _____ and (defeat) _____ the lead (run) _____ in the race.

9.   She (sew) _____ a button on her sweater after she had (wash) _____ it and (hang) _____ it out to dry.

ISBN: 978-1-897457-05-4

Reviewing New Words from the Passages

H. Fill in the blanks in the puzzle pairs using both the clues and the words listed below.

Puzzle Words to Match the Clues

evolved   propulsion   create   process   furious   speculate
excite   social   mastered   durable   predator   distinguish

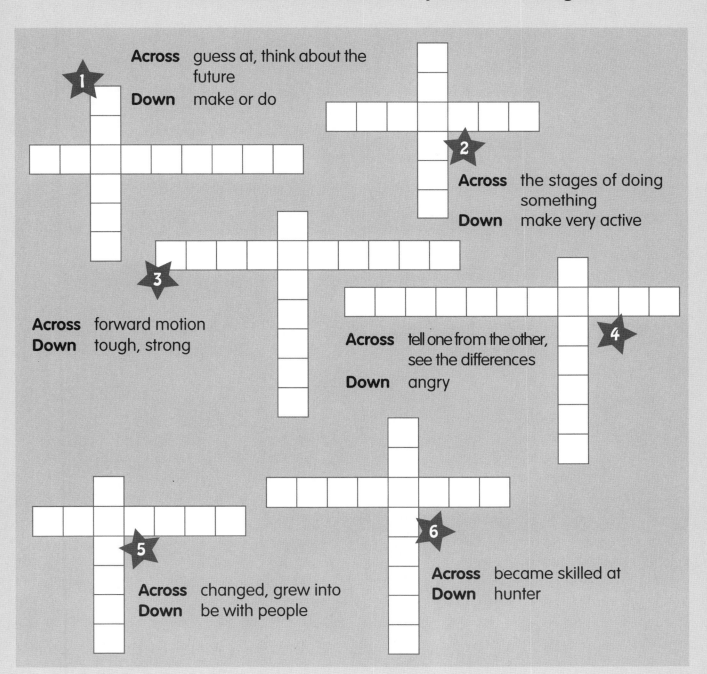

Across   guess at, think about the future
Down   make or do

Across   the stages of doing something
Down   make very active

Across   forward motion
Down   tough, strong

Across   tell one from the other, see the differences
Down   angry

Across   changed, grew into
Down   be with people

Across   became skilled at
Down   hunter

ISBN: 978-1-897457-05-4

ISBN: 978-1-897457-05-4

Outside

Inside

ISBN: 978-1-897457-05-4

unit 1 Nouns

Nouns

A **noun** names a person, an animal, a place, or a thing. It can be classified into one of the following types:

Countable common nouns – house, cat
Uncountable common nouns – water, air
Proper nouns – Trudeau, Michael
Compound proper nouns – Canadian Opera Company, National Ballet of Canada

A. Match the common nouns with the proper nouns by writing the letters in the correct circles.

A country
B street
C person
D city
E arena
F province
G book
H game
I continent
J park

WRITE THE LETTERS

1 Charlotte's Web
2 Manitoba
3 Queen's Park Crescent
4 Monopoly
5 Norway
6 South America
7 Chief Dan George
8 Montreal
9 Air Canada Centre
10 Stanley Park

ISBN: 978-1-897457-05-4

B. Read the passage and write the nouns in the table. Determine if they are countable common (CC), uncountable common (UC), proper (P), or compound proper (CP).

The city of Atlantis is one of the biggest mysteries. It is said that this ancient island vanished beneath the Atlantic Ocean "within a day and a night" about 12 000 years ago. Although this island may not have been real, it was described in great detail by Plato, a Greek philosopher. He wrote that Atlantis was given to Poseidon by Zeus. Life was good for many generations, but later, the people became corrupt. In Plato's story, Zeus decided to teach the people of Atlantis a lesson. Was this why the island vanished? Today, some people think Plato's story is not real. They think that he could have written in whatever way he desired because the island was fictional anyway.

1.	city	CC	2.		
3.			4.		
5.			6.		
7.			8.		
9.			10.		
11.			12.		
13.			14.		
15.			16.		
17.			18.		
19.			20.		

ISBN: 978-1-897457-05-4

Direct and Indirect Objects

A noun can be the object of a verb in a sentence. A **direct object** is the receiver of the action of the verb.

Example: Casey mailed the <u>package</u>.

An **indirect object** is to whom or what the action of the verb is directed.

Example: Casey mailed <u>Walter</u> the package.

C. Determine if each underlined object is direct "D" or indirect "I".

1.   The pianist played a wonderful <u>song</u>. _____

2.   Lucy ate the entire <u>cake</u> in the kitchen. _____

3.   May told her <u>mother</u> about the latest horror film. _____

4.   Bobby sends his buddy a <u>postcard</u> from Amsterdam. _____

5.   Janice lent <u>Wendy</u> her scooter. _____

D. Circle "D" if the sentence contains a direct object, "I" if it contains an indirect object, and "N" if it contains neither. You may circle "D" and "I" in some cases.

1.   Carly wore a pretty dress in the evening.   D | I | N

2.   Mrs. Robinson told Carly not to go out late at night.   D | I | N

3.   Sean read his daughter a bedtime story.   D | I | N

4.   Lynn ordered some gifts from an online company.   D | I | N

5.   Emma gives her dog delicious treats from time to time.   D | I | N

6.   The sweet music is playing in the lounge.   D | I | N

7.   Emma's dog catches the Frisbee with his big mouth.   D | I | N

8.   Bert lives a few blocks away.   D | I | N

ISBN: 978-1-897457-05-4

E.   Write the underlined words in the correct columns. You will find that most of the answers in the column for indirect objects are pronouns.

It was a dark and rainy night. Emily had just finished reading her <u>book</u> and wanted to get a <u>snack</u> from the kitchen. Other than her cat and the occasional field mouse, the house was empty. When Emily reached the <u>bottom of the staircase</u>, she saw a <u>mouse</u> scurrying around the corner. Normally, this would not have given <u>her</u> the <u>creeps</u>. But on this particular night, Emily had an eerie <u>feeling</u> that the mouse was trying to tell <u>her</u> <u>something</u>. What had it just seen? She felt a <u>wisp of air</u> over her head. "Deliciously scary" was how her best friend had always described this <u>house</u>. Emily turned around to see what had brought <u>home</u> the <u>wind</u>. To her disappointment, it was her <u>cat</u>. It had leapt from the staircase railing, wearing the <u>cape</u> that Emily had put on it earlier. "My house is never scary enough," she sighed, and opened the <u>cabinet</u> to get some cookies.

Direct Objects	**Indirect Objects**
book	

unit 2 Pronouns

Subject, Object, and Reflexive Pronouns

In a sentence or paragraph, the **subject pronoun** takes the place of the subject noun, and the **object pronoun** takes the place of the object noun. A **reflexive pronoun** is a type of object pronoun. We use it when the subject's action turns back on the subject.

Example: Susan likes apples. <u>She</u> likes <u>them</u> because <u>they</u> are sweet. <u>She</u> usually washes <u>herself</u> after a day at the farm.

A.   Determine if each underlined pronoun is a subject (S), an object (O), or a reflexive (R) pronoun. Write the question numbers in each group.

1.   "Could you take a picture of <u>me</u> next to this sculpture?" Sylvia asked Ted.

2.   Danny made a big breakfast for <u>himself</u>.

3.   Maggie taught <u>herself</u> how to roller-skate.

4.   Archie missed school yesterday because <u>he</u> was sick.

5.   My mother is a teacher. <u>She</u> teaches Drama and Music.

6.   <u>We</u> saw Stephen at the park yesterday, but he didn't see us.

7.   "Look at all these presents!" Tom exclaimed. "They're for <u>us</u>!"

8.   "Did you make these cards <u>yourself</u>?" Mrs. Robinson asked her son.

B. Choose the appropriate reflexive pronoun for each sentence.

themselves   ourselves   yourselves   herself
himself   myself   yourself   itself

1.   I wash _____ when I get up.

2.   Aaron got _____ into trouble.

3.   Megan set _____ an impossible task.

4.   The little mice hid _____ behind the piano.

5.   After we fell, we picked _____ up.

C. Fill in the blanks with the appropriate pronouns.

We often make the mistake of using "me" when we should be using "I", and vice versa. So pay close attention to the structure of the sentences as you do this exercise.

1.   There is a squirrel in the backyard.

_____ is burrowing its food in the ground.

2.   Jenny asked Carol, "Do you want to meet Betty and _____ at the restaurant? We can have dinner there together."

3.   Carol said, "Linda and _____ will be seeing a movie tonight. Sorry I won't be able to join you this time."

4.   "You don't have to thank me," said Jane to Darren. "These cookies are my thanks to _____ , actually."

5.   Little Gordon and little Terry are very tired. _____ have gone to bed.

> ## Demonstrative Pronouns
>
> When we want to identify people or point to physical objects, we use **"this"**, **"that"**, **"these"**, or **"those"**. When we want to refer to someone or something that has already been mentioned, or is known in the sentence, we use **"one"** or **"ones"**.
>
> *Examples*: <u>This</u> ice cream cone looks really good.
> "<u>That</u>'s no excuse," said Mother.
> <u>These</u> flowers over here are pretty.
> My budgie looks cuter than <u>those</u> over there.
> "I don't like jackets with zippers," says the customer. "Do you have <u>one</u> with buttons?"

D. Fill in the blanks with the appropriate demonstrative pronouns.

1. "I brought you _____ ," said Adam as he held out a bag of grapes.

2. "Look at _____ one," said Natalie, holding a grape between her fingers. "It's as big as a ping-pong ball!"

3. " _____ was an interesting story you just told, Dad!" Michael said.

4. "Are the new dresses longer than the old _____ ?" Clara asks.

5. The shirts on sale at this store are not the same _____ we saw at the other store.

6. "Who's _____ ?" Amanda asked the person on the line.

7. "Was _____ Aunt Meg on the phone?" Mother asked Amanda.

8. " _____ are my children – Jonathan and Emma," says Mrs. Lau, pointing at the kids playing in the sand far away.

ISBN: 978-1-897457-05-4

Relative Pronouns

Relative pronouns are those that relate to a previously occurring noun in the sentence.

Examples: This is the building <u>where</u> I work.
Let's meet on a day <u>when</u> we're both free.
This is the person <u>whom</u> I met.
This is the person <u>who</u> took me around the city.

E.   Complete each of the following sentences with the appropriate relative pronoun.

> when   where   whom   which   whose   that   who

1.   I want to see a movie _____ features polar bears.

2.   This is the place _____ we live.

3.   My cousins live in Iqaluit, _____ is the capital city of Nunavut.

4.   My brother is the person _____ help I always seek.

5.   Let's meet up for lunch on Wednesday _____ the restaurant is not crowded.

6.   The illustrator of this picture book is the one _____ I told you about.

7.   Susie wants to read a book _____ will blow her away.

8.   My grandma is the one in the family _____ always tells me stories.

Remember this:

"who", "whose", and "whom" relate to people; "which" and "that" relate to things.

> **Modal Verbs**
>
> We use "**can**" to talk about ability in the present or future.
>
> *Examples*: Patrick <u>can</u> play the piano, but Lucy <u>cannot</u>.
>
> "I <u>can't</u> babysit your brother today," says Shelley. "But I <u>can</u> tomorrow."
>
> We also use "**can**" to give or ask permission in the present or future.
>
> *Examples*: "<u>Can</u> we have a snack before we go to bed, Mom?" ask the children.
>
> "Okay. You <u>can</u> have a few cookies," says Mother.

A. Write "A" for ability and "P" for permission.

1. Beavers can build amazing dams. ____

2. "You're kidding me, Richard!" says Tom. "Beavers can't sing!" ____

3. "Sure, you can use my computer to surf the Web," says Michael to Todd. ____

4. Sydney's dog can read his owner's mind. ____

5. Bob cannot go to the baseball game tonight because he is grounded for a week. ____

6. Frankie is only five but he can already swim quite well. ____

7. "No, you cannot eat all the cookies in the jar," says Mother. ____

8. You can drive to Germany from France, but you cannot do that from Australia. ____

ISBN: 978-1-897457-05-4

We use "**could**" to talk about ability or permission in the past.

Examples: Leila <u>could</u> talk when she was barely two.
Julie <u>could not</u> talk until she was almost three.
The teacher just told the class that they <u>could</u> do some silent reading.

We also use "**could**" to talk about possibility.

Examples: "Why isn't Tim in class today?" asks Jon.
"He <u>could</u> be sick," said Lewis.
"Look how dark it is outside," says Bob. "It <u>could</u> start raining any minute."

B.   Determine whether each of the following is about ability, permission, or possibility.   Write the correct question numbers in the spaces provided.

1.   "The bell could ring any minute now," says Mr. Graham.

2.   Grandpa could read four newspapers in one afternoon back in the days when he was young.

3.   Jeremiah asked his parents if he could have the last piece of pie.

4.   Melissa said I could borrow her books when she finished reading them.

5.   The line-up was so crowded yesterday that nobody could move even an inch.

6.   Christopher could juggle three balls when he worked at the circus.

7.   I doubt the corner store will close down, but of course I could be wrong.

8.   There could be a storm tomorrow, as forecast by the Weather Network.

We use **"will"**, **"would"**, and **"could"** to ask for assistance in a polite way.

Examples: "Would you please deliver this box to 30 Maple Avenue?" the shop owner asked Bob.
"Yes. Certainly," Bob replied.
"Could you open the door for me?" Bob asked Pam at the entrance.
"Yes, of course," said Pam. "Will you buy some stationery on your way back?"
"Sure," said Bob.

C. Complete the following dialogues by using "will", "would", or "could" to form polite questions. Choose the appropriate key phrase for each one.

1. Victor: I'm trying to study, Bill.

   _____

   _____

   Bill: Oh yes. Sorry. I'll turn it down.

help me open the windows
pick up the phone for me
turn the stereo down a bit
pick up a few cartons

2. Mrs. Gladwin: There's no more milk in the fridge.

   _____

   _____

   Mr. Gladwin: Sure. No problem.

3. Jessica: The phone is ringing, but my hands are full.

   _____

   Gregory: Of course.

4. Mrs. Kemp: It's getting hot in the classroom.

   _____

   Vicki: Sure.

ISBN: 978-1-897457-05-4

D. Ask a polite question with "will", "would", or "could" for each scenario below.

"Could" is more polite than "can" because "could" suggests possibility, while "can" is definite – we use it to talk about ability and permission. By using "could" to ask for assistance, we give the other person "more room" to think about our request.

1. A group of children are playing in the yard and their ball went over the fence. They see someone walking by. One of the children asks:

   _____

2. Susan Abrams wants to talk to her mother. She calls her mother's office and the secretary picks up the phone. Susan asks the secretary:

   _____

3. It is dinner time. Mark wants some ketchup for his chicken fingers. The ketchup bottle is next to his sister Chelsea. Mark asks Chelsea:

   _____

4. The doorbell just rang. Except Marie, everyone is busy doing something. Mother asks Marie:

   _____

5. Carol wants to visit the shoe museum after school, and wants her sister, Jenny, to take the subway with her. She asks Jenny:

   _____

> **Present Tense: Simple and Progressive**
>
> We use the **simple present tense** when talking about a habit or a simple truth.
>
> *Example*:   Jim <u>has</u> a glass of milk every morning.
>
> We use the **present progressive tense** when talking about an action that is going on, or an action that will take place in the near future.
>
> *Examples*:   Jennifer <u>is wrapping</u> presents for her friends.
>   Shelby <u>is coming</u> tomorrow.

A.   Fill in the blanks with the present progressive tense of the verbs in parentheses.

Watch your spelling of the verbs in the progressive tense.

1.   Nicki (show) _____ Jack her new running shoes.

2.   The children (run) _____ towards the ice cream truck.

3.   The breeze (blow) _____ through the trees.

4.   The dog (chew) _____ on a new toy in the family room.

5.   Jack (go) _____ down the stairs on his pogo stick.

6.   Mom and Dad (prepare) _____ dinner together this evening.

7.   The soup (simmer) _____ in the pot.

8.   A firefly (shine) _____ in the dark.

9.   The fire (burn) _____ brightly in the fireplace.

ISBN: 978-1-897457-05-4

B. Fill in the blanks with the simple present or present progressive tense of the verbs in parentheses.

1. Bernie (sing) _____ a pretty song every morning.

2. Jan (think) _____ about what to include on her party menu.

3. Shelby (look) _____ after her baby sister whenever her mother is out.

4. Janice (like) _____ her aunt's beautiful vase.

5. Sara (plan) _____ to visit Calgary in July.

6. I (arrive) _____ by train tonight.

7. Mrs. Watt (read) _____ her son a bedtime story every night.

8. Bobby (give) _____ his dog a bath once every three weeks.

C. Use the keywords correctly to write one sentence in the simple present tense and one in the present progressive tense.

1. farmers   milk   cows   now   day

   a. _____

   b. _____

2. children   lie   meadow   afternoon

   a. _____

   b. _____

3. Daphne   Sophia   fall   asleep   television   night

   a. _____

   b. _____

> ## Past Tense: Simple and Progressive
>
> We use the **simple past tense** when talking about something that happened habitually or at a particular time in the past.
>
> *Examples*:   Craig <u>woke</u> up early yesterday.
> Wendy <u>lived</u> in Montreal for five months last year.
>
> We often use the **past progressive tense** when talking about something that continued to happen over a period of time.
>
> *Example*:   Aidan <u>was watching</u> TV when the doorbell rang.

D. Fill in the blanks with the simple past or past progressive tense of the verbs in parentheses.

1. Fabio (fly) _____ in his dream when his cat woke him up.

2. Cassandra's friends often (talk) _____ to her when she was trying to study.

3. Martin (walk) _____ to the library when he bumped into an old friend from kindergarten.

4. Margaret (rehearse) _____ with her choir when she was called to the office.

5. Wayne often (play) _____ catch with his buddies last summer.

6. The telephone rang when I (take) _____ a shower.

7. The teachers (have) _____ a meeting yesterday.

8. Keith was debating whether to get a banana split or a strawberry sundae when he (spot) _____ a chocolate fudge sandwich on the menu and (decide) _____ to order that instead.

ISBN: 978-1-897457-05-4

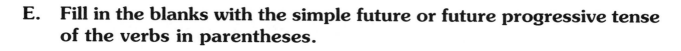

Future Tense: Simple and Progressive

We use the **simple future tense** when talking about something that will happen.

Examples: It <u>will be</u> warm and sunny tomorrow.
Richard <u>will rest</u> after mowing the lawn.

We use the **future progressive tense** when talking about something that will happen over a period of time.

Examples: Richard <u>will be napping</u> for the rest of the day.
The sun <u>will be shining</u> for the entire afternoon.

E.   Fill in the blanks with the simple future or future progressive tense of the verbs in parentheses.

1.   Many of us (watch) _____ the parade on TV.

2.   The phone (ring) _____ in five minutes.

3.   Vinnie's cousin (visit) _____ for the summer.

4.   There (be) _____ a new radio program on Monday morning.

5.   Shelley (ride) _____ her bicycle to school this year.

6.   Marty (attend) _____ a different school for some time.

7.   Catherine's children (play) _____ one more game.

8.   Since the day is so hot, they (swim) _____ until sunset.

9.   The Lings (drive) _____ to Florida in March.

unit 5 Verbs (3)

> ### Voice: Active and Passive
>
> We use the **active voice** when we want to talk about a person or thing doing something.
>
> *Example*:   Neil built a dog house yesterday.
>
> We use the **passive voice** when we want to focus on the person or thing **affected by** something.
>
> *Example*:   A dog house was built yesterday.

A. **Write "passive" or "active" on the lines to indicate whether the sentences are in passive or active voice.**

1. Jason played with his dog in the backyard.   _____

2. The dishes were washed after the table was cleared.   _____

3. Dinner was served later than expected.   _____

4. Jane bought a new purse while she was in Montreal.   _____

5. New shoes were also purchased by Jane.   _____

6. Manny walked over to Dominic's house.   _____

7. The director explained the script to the actors.   _____

8. The story was read to the children before bedtime.   _____

9. Rebecca was driven to school by her father.

    _____

10. The teacher gave the students more time to work on their assignments.

    _____

ISBN: 978-1-897457-05-4

B. Rewrite each of the following sentences in the passive voice. The first one is done for you.

> When using the passive voice, we often don't mention the person or thing that performs the action.

1. Mother sewed a flower on Charmaine's bag.

   A flower was sewn on Charmaine's bag.

   _____

2. Mother tied Charmaine's hair with ribbons.

   _____

3. Charmaine checked her bag.

   _____

4. The passengers boarded the airplane.

   _____

5. The flight attendants showed the passengers their seats.

   _____

6. The flight attendant put Charmaine's bag in the overhead compartment.

   _____

7. More passengers filled the overhead compartments with bags.

   _____

8. The passengers placed their seats in upright positions.

   _____

9. The pilot prepared the plane for take-off.

   _____

C. **Rewrite each of the following sentences in the active voice. The subject is given for you.**

1. The seatbelts were unfastened.

   The passengers _____ .

2. Passengers were served light snacks on the plane.

   The flight attendants _____ .

3. The passengers were told there would be a delay.

   The pilot _____ .

4. The washrooms were not occupied yet.

   No one _____ .

5. Charmaine was given some paper and crayons.

   A flight attendant _____ .

6. A cute airplane was drawn.

   Charmaine _____ .

7. The passengers were asked if they would like a drink.

   The flight attendants _____ .

8. Newspapers were handed out.

   The flight attendants _____

   _____ .

Changing from the active to the passive and vice versa represents a shift in the point of view.

9. Clouds could be seen through the windows.

   Charmaine _____

   _____ .

10. Charmaine was given a choice of meals.

    The flight attendant _____

    _____ .

ISBN: 978-1-897457-05-4

D. With verbs that can take two objects, we can form two different passive sentences. Write each of the following passive sentences in a different way. The first one is done for you.

1. Charmaine was given a meal of pasta with meatballs.

   A meal of pasta with meatballs was given to Charmaine.

2. Some extra napkins were handed to the passengers.

   _____

3. The passengers were shown a movie.

   _____

4. Earphones for the audio system were given to the passengers.

   _____

5. The safety precautions were told to the passengers.

   _____

6. The passengers were provided with the weather report.

   _____

7. Desserts and drinks were offered to the passengers.

   _____

   _____

8. The bag was handed to Charmaine after the plane had landed.

   _____

   _____

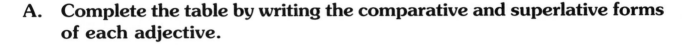

unit 6 Adjectives and Adverbs

Comparative and Superlative Adjectives

We use **comparative adjectives** to compare two people, animals, things, or groups. We use **superlative adjectives** when the comparison is among three or more.

Examples: The giraffe's neck is <u>longer</u> than Susie's.
            The giraffe has the <u>longest</u> neck among animals.

A. **Complete the table by writing the comparative and superlative forms of each adjective.**

	Adjective	Comparative	Superlative
1.	safe		
2.	happy		happiest
3.	forgetful	more forgetful	
4.	great		
5.	big	bigger	
6.	friendly		
7.	sad		
8.	nice		
9.	important		most important
10.	thin		
11.	influential		
12.	easy		
13.	tiny		
14.	marvellous		

ISBN: 978-1-897457-05-4

B. **Check if the comparative or superlative adjective in each sentence is in the correct form. If not, write the correct form on the line.**

1. Marie's room is the most tidy. _____

2. We had the splendidest dinner in Little Italy. _____

3. Kim's mother makes the smoothest cheesecake. _____

4. There is another restaurant further down the street. _____

5. Todd is the most happy boy when it is summer.

    _____

6. We think soccer is funner than baseball.

    _____

C. **Use the following keywords to write sentences with comparative or superlative adjectives.**

1. Doris   bustling   Toronto   Canada   thinks   city

    _____

2. Jill   Jack   careful   than   person

    _____

3. Kelly   Dana   usually   than   fast

    _____

4. beautiful   Rome   Paris   city   than

    _____

5. Judy   class   girl   tall

    _____

ISBN: 978-1-897457-05-4

Creating Adjectives from Verbs

Many verbs can become adjectives when we add "**ing**" or "**ed**" to them. In general, "-ing" adjectives describe the effect of someone or something, while "-ed" adjectives describe someone's feelings.

Examples: Lori's skipping ability is <u>amazing</u>.
Her friends were <u>amazed</u> when they were skipping during recess.

D. Create adjectives from the following verbs to complete the table.

	-ing	-ed
1. charm	1.	
2. annoy	2.	
3. frighten	3.	
4. embarrass	4.	
5. bore	5.	
6. welcome	6.	
7. move	7.	

E. Choose an appropriate adjective from the table above to complete each sentence.

1. Clara looked _____ when she saw a bat.

2. The student was so _____ that he fell asleep.

3. My little sister whines in an _____ voice.

4. Richard lives in a _____ house with a cute fence.

5. I wept at the end of the film because the story was so _____ .

Comparative and Superlative Adverbs

Comparative and **superlative adverbs** are formed and used in the same way as comparative and superlative adjectives.

Examples: The audience arrived <u>sooner</u> than expected.
The smallest puppy barked <u>the loudest</u> out of all the puppies in the litter.

F. Choose the most appropriate adverb and use it in the comparative or superlative form for each sentence.

soon   early
usually   frequently
often   late

1. The _____ we arrive, the less time we will have to explore the city.

2. The _____ Marla gets better, the faster she could resume training.

3. Terry has been visiting his grandpa _____ over the past two weeks.

4. Sam is like a bird. Of everyone in his family, he always gets up _____ .

5. Sometimes he will get a coffee, or even a hot chocolate, but he orders tea _____ .

6. Because of the strange circumstances, the principal took the students on the field trip. It is _____ the teacher who takes them.

A. Read the story. Underline the countable common nouns and circle the uncountable common nouns.

The Garcias want to take a vacation. Mr. and Mrs. Garcia decide to take their son, Ivan, and their daughter, Marissa, camping in Sandbanks Provincial Park in Ontario. The family has taken a few vacations before but this will be their first time camping together. In fact, only Mr. Garcia has camped before.

Mr. Garcia starts to pack the car. The most important item is the tent. He packs clothing, sleeping bags, fishing gear, pillows, insect repellent, sunscreen, and games. Mrs. Garcia hands him a cooler and the water.

While he fits everything into the car, Mr. Garcia sends Ivan and Marissa back into the house a few times. "Where we are going, you will not need those," he says as he hands Ivan his video games. "You won't need these either," he says to Marissa as he passes her the movies she wanted to bring.

"What will we do there?" Ivan asks.

"You'll see," says Mr. Garcia. "Now hurry up. You are taking too much time."

Ivan and Marissa wonder if they will have any fun on this trip.

ISBN: 978-1-897457-05-4

B. Write the seven proper nouns included in the passage.

1. _____   2. _____

3. _____   4. _____

5. _____   6. _____

7. _____

Which of these is a compound proper noun?

8. _____

C. Write "D" or "I" to indicate whether the underlined words are direct or indirect objects.

1. Mr. Garcia drives the <u>car</u>. ____

2. Mrs. Garcia turns on the <u>radio</u>. ____

3. Mrs. Garcia sings <u>Mr. Garcia</u> a song. ____

4. Ivan lends <u>Marissa</u> a magazine for the car ride. ____

5. The Garcias eat <u>sandwiches</u> at a rest stop. ____

6. Mrs. Garcia gives <u>Ivan</u> a book to read.

____

7. Marissa shares her box of <u>cookies</u> with Ivan.

____

8. Marissa takes a <u>nap</u> in the car on the way.

____

D. Fill in the blanks with the correct pronouns (subject, object, reflexive, demonstrative, or relative).

> us   herself   which   we   she   he
> themselves   this   him   they

The Garcias arrive at the campground and find their campsite,

1. _____ is right on the lake. Mr. Garcia begins to set up the tent.

2. _____ asks Ivan and Marissa to help.

Mr. Garcia tells Ivan to go fishing with 3. _____ early the next morning. Ivan is not very happy about 4. _____ . "Why do 5. _____ have to get up so early during our vacation?" Ivan whines to his father.

"Because that's when the fish will be ready for 6. _____ ," Mr. Garcia says sternly. "Now let's gather some firewood." Ivan and Marissa look at each other with wide eyes. 7. _____ are both thinking the same thing – this vacation seems to be more about work than having fun!

The family works hard to gather firewood. Ivan and Marissa are not having a good time. Marissa even pretends to trip and hurt 8. _____ ! Mr. and Mrs. Garcia can tell that 9. _____ is not really hurt.

After collecting enough wood, Mr. Garcia tells Ivan and Marissa that they are allowed to go and play. Suddenly, they realize that they don't have any of the things they play with at home. Ivan and Marissa don't know what to do with 10. _____ .

ISBN: 978-1-897457-05-4

E. Underline the modal verb in each sentence. Write the number under "ability", "permission", or "possibility" to show the function of the modal verb below.

1. "Yes, you two can do what you wish," says Mr. Garcia.

2. Ivan could not remember the last time he went swimming with Marissa.

3. "We could go swimming," suggests Ivan.

4. Marissa cannot swim very well.

5. "Can you think of something else to do?" asks Marissa.

6. "You can't miss dinner," Mrs. Garcia calls after them.

Ability | Permission | Possibility

F. Rewrite the sentences from the simple present tense into the present progressive tense.

1. Ivan and Marissa walk along the beach.

_____

2. The wind blows gently.

_____

3. Ivan wears his sandals.

_____

4. Marissa wishes she could watch a movie.

_____

5. Ivan thinks about his favourite video game.

_____

G. Fill in the blank by changing the verb in parentheses to the tense indicated under each sentence.

1. Marissa (feel) _____ bored and tired.
   Future progressive

2. "I (rest) _____ for a little while," she says.
   Simple future

3. Ivan (suggest) _____ they run.
   Simple present

4. They (run) _____ as fast as they could.
   Past progressive

5. "I (see) _____ something by that rock," says Ivan.
   Simple past

H. Write "active" or "passive" to indicate which voice is used in each sentence.

1. Ivan sees something that looks interesting. _____

2. The children approach the rock excitedly. _____

3. Marissa is shown the rock. _____

4. Ivan carefully examines the object. _____

5. The object is picked up.

   _____

6. They see that it is a brass bottle that looks very old.

   _____

7. The bottle is taken back to the campsite by Ivan and Marissa.

   _____

ISBN: 978-1-897457-05-4

I. Read the passage. Fill in the blanks with the correct comparative or superlative adjectives.

> shiniest   sillier   faster   more important
> most popular   most interesting   prettier

Ivan and Marissa rush back to the campsite. They run very fast but Ivan is a bit 1._____ than Marissa. They cannot wait to show the bottle to their parents. Everyone finds the bottle interesting and they agree that it is the 2._____ bottle they have ever seen.

Ivan sets the bottle on the picnic table. "That bottle is so pretty! It is much 3._____ than this one!" says Mrs. Garcia as she pours a glass of pop from an ordinary plastic bottle. The brass bottle glistens in the sunshine. "It's also the 4._____ bottle of all the bottles we own," she says.

The family discusses where the bottle might have come from. Marissa has a silly idea that it fell from the sky but Mr. Garcia's idea that it magically appeared on the beach is 5._____ . A popular idea is that it was left here by someone but the 6._____ one is that it washed upon the shore.

Everyone is very excited about the discovery. Ivan and Marissa want to spend more time figuring out the mystery of the brass bottle, but Mr. and Mrs. Garcia think having dinner is 7._____ right now.

ISBN: 978-1-897457-05-4

Conjunctions

A **conjunction** is a word that joins together words, phrases, or sentences.

Example: Mr. Saber is a happy <u>and</u> fun-loving farmer. <u>Although</u> he is well into his fifties, he is like a kid at times. His wife wants him to grow up, <u>but</u> he prefers to be young at heart.

A.   Circle the conjunctions in the following sentences.

1.   Marie and Joseph arrived before Mrs. Saber had time to clean up the house.

2.   Mrs. Johnston waited at the station until the sun went down.

3.   The children left the beach only after it had started to rain.

4.   Mrs. Morgan called to her son, "You're not going to be on time unless you hurry up!"

5.   To get to Vancouver from Toronto, we can travel by plane or train.

6.   The little kid said to his dad at the park, "Catch me if you can!"

7.   Although the seats were not very comfortable on the train, Mrs. Simmons did not complain.

8.   Mr. Saber is in a very good mood today because his favourite hen has laid a few eggs.

9.   Mr. Saber has been a farmer since he was fifteen years old.

10.   Catherine arrived at the train station and was so happy to see Wendy.

B. Fill in the blanks with the appropriate conjunctions.

because	unless	therefore
while	still	than	although
so	since	but	when	if

1. Marie and Joseph did not want to leave _____ they would miss the animals on the farm.

2. Mrs. Saber did not like the roast she prepared, _____ everyone else enjoyed it.

3. Mr. and Mrs. Saber will not move to the city _____ there is a very good reason to do so.

4. _____ Marie and Joseph are city dwellers, they _____ visit their grandparents' farm every now and then.

5. Marie and Joseph will come back to the farm next weekend _____ the weather is nice.

6. The hen went back to sleep _____ Mr. Saber was not looking.

7. Marie and Joseph got stuck in traffic on their way back to the city; _____ , they might be late getting home.

8. Marie and Joseph had forgotten that it was a long weekend, _____ they didn't need to rush home after all.

ISBN: 978-1-897457-05-4

C. Some conjunctions are used in pairs. Complete each sentence with the appropriate pair.

> either...or   neither...nor   not only...but also
> both...and   whether...or

1. Canada is _not only_ a big country _but also_ very cold in winter.

2. Carly said to Mel, "_____ you are mistaken _____ I am."

3. The students in Mrs. Peters's class _____ love _____ respect her.

4. The Simpsons do not mind _____ they stay _____ move to another house.

5. "Things are _____ good _____ bad; only thinking makes them so," a teacher said to Bob, who had a puzzled look on his face.

6. It doesn't matter _____ it rains tomorrow _____ if it is sunny; we will still go to the party.

7. Tomorrow is _____ my birthday _____ Mira's birthday.

8. It is _____ necessary _____ is it a good idea to go out in that terrible storm.

9. The musicians are _____ excited _____ nervous about their concert later this evening.

D. Combine the sentences into one using a suitable conjunction.

1. You can run. You can't hide.

   _____

2. Maggie will meet us at the skating rink. It is close to her house.

   _____

3. Tristan didn't finish his homework last night. He won't be able to go to the fair with us.

   _____

4. The blue team didn't win. They put forth their best effort.

   _____

5. Darryl didn't like the restaurant. Next time, he will eat somewhere else.

   _____

6. Mrs. Bryant bought three packages of cookies. They were on sale.

   _____

7. Allison and Peter didn't like the restaurant. They are going to give it another try.

   _____

   _____

   _____

8. Hiking in the woods is fun. It is also good for you.

   _____

   _____

   _____

unit 8 Phrases

Noun Phrases

A **noun phrase** functions like a noun in a sentence. It can be the subject, object, or the complement *. It can simply be one or more nouns, or a combination of nouns and other words like adjectives.

Example: Little Ashley (subject) is building <u>a big snowman</u>
(object), which is <u>her first snowman</u> (complement)
this winter.

* A complement is a noun phrase which follows "am", "is", or "are".

A. Decide whether each underlined noun phrase is the subject (S), object (O), or complement (C).

1. <u>Lindsay and her mom</u> have just gone into a new grocery store.   _____

2. The things they need to buy are <u>bread, some deli meats, snacks, and detergent</u>.   _____

3. Lindsay wants to get <u>a pack of salad mix</u>.   _____

4. Lindsay also wants some chocolate ice cream because it is <u>her favourite ice cream</u>.   _____

5. Lindsay's mom tells Lindsay that in the fridge at home are <u>some chopped up cauliflower sticks</u>.   _____

6. The cheerful cashier hands Lindsay's mom <u>some brand new dollar bills</u> as change, which Lindsay wants to add to her collection.   _____

7. Lindsay returns <u>the shopping cart</u> to the front of the store.   _____

8. <u>Lindsay's mom</u> thinks she will definitely come to this new grocery store again.   _____

ISBN: 978-1-897457-05-4

Adjective and Adverb Phrases

An **adjective phrase** functions like an adjective in a sentence. It describes a noun.

Example: Megan has a <u>very big</u> smile on her face because she just got a <u>cute and cuddly</u> teddy bear for her birthday.

An **adverb phrase** functions like an adverb in a sentence. It describes a verb.

Example: Megan's brother thinks his sister is <u>too easily</u> pleased. He thinks the teddy bear is <u>rather poorly</u> made.

B. **Decide whether each underlined phrase is an adjective or adverb phrase by writing the correct question numbers in the boxes.**

1. Jason can build <u>tall and impressive</u> towers with cards.

2. He can build them <u>so quickly</u> that he amazes his friends.

3. Sometimes, he can finish building a tower <u>quite comfortably</u> in five minutes.

4. On occasion, Jason will get up <u>unusually early</u> to engage in his new hobby.

5. The towers that Jason built are always <u>incredibly sturdy</u>.

6. Jason's friends can't understand how the <u>light and flimsy</u> cards can stand like that.

7. The trick to building towers with cards, Jason says, is to put down each card <u>very swiftly but carefully</u>.

8. Jason thinks his new hobby is <u>fun and interesting</u>.

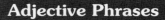

Adjective Phrases

Adverb Phrases

Infinitive Phrases

An **infinitive phrase** contains a verb that follows "to".

Examples: Little Ben crawls toward his sister <u>to hold her hand</u>.
Candace reaches out <u>to grab her brother's hand</u>.

C.   Underline the infinitive phrase in each of the following sentences.

1.   Rachel and her cousins woke up early this Saturday morning to go to the amusement park.

2.   They arrived at the park before most people to be among the first in line for their rides.

3.   Both Rachel and her younger cousin Kim are tall enough to ride on the roller-coaster.

4.   After the thrill of the roller-coaster, Rachel and Kim got ready to try the Swing of the Millennium.

5.   Meanwhile, Rachel's other cousins Michelle and Liz were a bit hungry and ran off to get some food.

6.   Since Kim loves horses, Rachel went with her to ride on the carousel.

7.   Rachel thought the Spinning Octopus looked quite amazing, and walked over to look at the design.

8.   Kim found a bench to sit down on.

9.   Michelle and Liz came back to share some French fries with Rachel and Kim.

Gerund Phrases

A **gerund phrase** contains a verb in the "-ing" form. It can function as the subject, object, complement, or the object of preposition in a sentence.

Examples: <u>Playing softball</u> is a game we all enjoy. (subject)
Jim likes <u>playing softball</u> with his buddies. (object)
The greatest joy is <u>playing softball</u>. (complement)
Jim is excellent at <u>playing softball</u>. (object of preposition)

D. Identify each underlined gerund phrase as subject (S), object (O), complement (C), or object of preposition (P).

1. Marla is not very good at <u>preparing meals</u>.   ____

2. Jack enjoys <u>playing street hockey</u> with his neighbours.   ____

3. Amanda's favourite activity is <u>spending long holidays</u> at the family cottage.   ____

4. <u>Reading storybooks</u> is one of the best things to do in spare time.   ____

E. Choose the appropriate gerund phrase for each sentence.

> playing sports of all kinds   forgiving your siblings
> waiting for her turn   biting nails

1. Kevin is very athletic. He enjoys _____ .

2. _____ is one of Jane's bad habits, but she has made a resolution to get rid of it this year.

3. _____ for their mistakes is not hard to do.

4. Though the line-ups at the food court are long, Sadie does not mind _____ to order.

unit 9 Clauses

Independent and Dependent Clauses

An **independent clause** can function as a complete sentence.

Example: <u>A monster appeared in the movie</u> and <u>the children screamed</u>.
                          (independent)   (independent)

A **dependent clause** cannot function as a complete sentence. It needs an independent clause to make its meaning complete.

Example: <u>Though the monster disappeared</u>, <u>the children kept screaming</u>.
                          (dependent)   (independent)

A. Write "I" in the circle if the underlined clause is independent; write "D" if it is dependent.

1. <u>When it is nice outside</u>, Gabriel likes to climb trees.   ◯

2. <u>Zadie likes riding her bicycle</u>.   ◯

3. <u>When spring arrives</u>, Marie will plant lots of flowers.   ◯

4. <u>When are you arriving</u>?   ◯

5. Before you leave, <u>remember to pack a sweater in the suitcase</u>.   ◯

6. <u>How much are these nectarines</u>?   ◯

7. <u>You can mail the card</u>.   ◯

8. <u>If we go there early in the morning</u>, we could avoid the crowds.   ◯

9. The children all went out to play <u>because it was a sunny day</u>.   ◯

10. <u>The girls did better than the boys in this year's spelling bee</u>.   ◯

ISBN: 978-1-897457-05-4

B. **Add an independent clause to make a sentence with each of the following.**

1. Wesley went trick-or-treating and _____

_____ .

2. If you want to go to town, _____

_____ .

3. Since the train did not come on time, _____

_____ .

4. While we were waiting for the movie to start, _____

_____ .

5. The café was full of people because _____

_____ .

C. **Using the given conjunction, add a dependent clause to make a sentence with each of the following.**

1. because   We did not arrive in town on time _____

_____ .

2. while   Linda practised shooting the ball _____

_____ .

3. whenever   The restaurants are packed _____

_____ .

4. before   Mrs. Lionel's neighbours washed their car _____

_____ .

5. after   The teacher went to the basketball practice _____

_____ .

ISBN: 978-1-897457-05-4

Adjectival and Adverbial Clauses

An **adjectival clause** gives information about a noun in a sentence.

Example: The children, <u>who are back in the classroom now</u>, are making paintings.
"Who are back in the classroom now" gives information about "the children".

An **adverbial clause** tells where or when the action of a verb takes place.

Example: The football players did not arrive <u>until the stadium was packed</u>.
"Until the stadium was packed" tells when the football players arrived.

D. Write "adj" or "adv" for each underlined clause.

1. The children played at the park <u>before they went home</u>. _____

2. The food, <u>which had gone bad in the fridge</u>, has been thrown away. _____

3. Benny put the book back <u>where he found it</u>. _____

4. Mr. Lo went into the staff room <u>after he had dismissed his students</u>. _____

5. The children in Mr. Adam's class do well <u>whenever there is a pop quiz</u>. _____

6. The little geese follow Mr. Hillside <u>wherever he goes</u>. _____

7. Tom is the one <u>who always knows what to do</u>. _____

8. <u>After we had finished our homework</u>, we played catch in the field. _____

9. My cousin, <u>who comes from Prince George</u>, is enjoying her stay. _____

10. The train, <u>which is being stalled</u>, will not arrive for a while. _____

11. <u>Before we had our snacks</u>, we all went swimming. _____

12. My uncle will not arrive <u>until nine o'clock tonight</u>. _____

ISBN: 978-1-897457-05-4

E. Rewrite each of the following sentences by adding an adjectival clause.

1. This yo-yo is my sister's.

   _____

   _____

2. This boy is my son.

   _____

3. That book is my cousin's favourite.

   _____

4. The team played very well.

   _____

5. The newspapers are a mess.

   _____

F. Rewrite each of the following sentences by adding an adverbial clause.

1. The rabbits are having a race.

   _____

   _____

2. Ben and June said hello.

   _____

3. Jennifer is slowing down.

   _____

4. Bus 53 will not leave.

   _____

Simple Sentences

A **simple sentence** is formed whenever there is a subject and a verb.

Examples: Randy took out the garbage.
                The dog chased the cat.

A. **Check the groups of words that form simple sentences.**

1. The lazy cat. _____

2. Jennifer walks quickly. _____

3. He was late. _____

4. Catherine's pencil. _____

5. Leaving here. _____

6. The sun will rise. _____

7. Skiing in winter. _____

8. We drove through Georgia. _____

9. I'll ask. _____

10. Hot fudge sundaes. _____

B. **Rewrite two of the unchecked groups in (A), making them simple sentences.**

1. _____

2. _____

Compound Sentences

A **compound sentence** has two or more independent clauses.

Example: <u>Randy took out the garbage</u> but <u>he forgot the recycling bin</u>.

C.   Combine each of the given clauses with one from the list to make a compound sentence.

the teams will play tomorrow
I have to be home by 5 p.m.
we will visit our friends
he wouldn't hurt a flea
they are proud of their high marks
I will have to walk to school

1.   He's as strong as an ox but

_____ .

2.   I can go shopping tomorrow but

_____ .

3.   I need to catch the next bus or

_____ .

4.   Adam and Andrew studied very hard for their test and

_____ .

5.   The baseball game was cancelled today but

_____ .

6.   We will watch a movie tonight or

_____ .

> ## Complex Sentences
>
> A **complex sentence** has an independent clause and one or more dependent clauses.
>
> *Example*:   Randy took out the garbage because it is collection day tomorrow.
>   (independent)   (dependent)

D. Using the given conjunction, add a dependent clause to each of the following to make a complex sentence.

1. **after**   Wanda adopted a dog _____

   _____

   _____ .

2. **before**   Wendy finished her new book _____

   _____ .

3. **because**   Cherie wants a new pair of sneakers _____

   _____ .

4. **since**   Lily and Jo have known each other _____

   _____ .

5. **so**   Mrs. Stow did not want to cook today, _____

   _____ .

6. **because**   Mel and Joey did not see the movie yesterday _____

   _____ .

7. **while**   We play games in the doctor's office _____

   _____ .

ISBN: 978-1-897457-05-4

E. **Count the number of independent clauses in each of the following sentences. Write the number on the line.**

1. Fabio likes tuna but he does not like it in mayonnaise. _____

2. Rory likes tuna and he likes salmon, but he does not like them hot. _____

3. Molly did not want to wear a dress at first, but she changed her mind later. _____

4. Sara and Julie both like strawberry ice cream, but only Julie likes buying it from the ice cream truck. _____

5. Craig has just gone out and he will return in a few minutes, but he will have to head back out soon for a softball practice. _____

F. **Classify the following sentences by writing the question numbers in the correct spaces.**

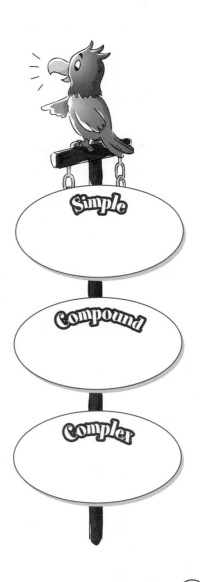

1. Robert likes to go swimming in the morning.

2. I will go if she invites me.

3. Carrie has a very chatty parrot.

4. Florence was named after her mother.

5. Mike would rather eat olives than pickles.

6. Gabrielle has been collecting stamps since she was six.

7. Lois will arrive today and she will leave the following Sunday.

8. Jenna likes playing in the band but she does not like morning rehearsals.

Punctuation

> ### Commas
>
> We use the **comma** (**,**) to indicate one or more pauses in a sentence.
>
> *Examples*: Giraffes, raccoons, and dolphins are all mammals.
> Clara, could you give me your phone number?
>
> If a sentence ending in a period is put inside quotation marks, replace the period with a comma.
>
> *Example*: "We are going out for dinner," said Dad.

A. Add commas to the sentences where appropriate.

1. Samantha Jacquelyn and Grace went to the concert together.

2. Kevin can you please help me?

3. Mom Dad and I are going to visit Toronto Montreal and Halifax this summer.

4. Pepper my dog knows a lot of tricks.

5. "I am going for a walk" said Taylor.

6. He wore a thick furry coat because it was cold outside.

7. Dad went to get eggs milk cheese and butter.

8. Natasha likes to play tennis read and paint.

9. Toby please set the table.

10. "We will go to the museum on Sunday" said Gregory.

ISBN: 978-1-897457-05-4

B. Rewrite the sentences using colons where appropriate.

Birthday List:
1. Telescope
2. Drawing pencils
3. New dress

1. Sherry has three items on her birthday list a telescope, drawing pencils, and a new dress.

   _____

   _____

2. There was one problem with Robert's plan he didn't have enough money to buy the material.

   _____

   _____

3. Never take school for granted some children in poor countries never get the chance to attend.

   _____

   _____

4. There are four foods Stephanie doesn't like to eat beans, pork, salmon, and bananas.

   _____

   _____

> ### Semicolons
>
> The **semicolon** (*;*) also indicates a pause in a sentence. It is used to join two separate sentences when the second elaborates on the first. It is also used to replace conjunctions such as "and", "but", "since", and "so".
>
> *Examples*: Our prices are wrong; we ordered from the old catalogue.
> Three people built the model; only one took credit for it.

C. Add semicolons to the sentences where appropriate.

1. Daisy said she will be late for dinner she has an appointment.

2. Tomorrow it will rain it will be good for the garden.

3. We cannot wait much longer we will miss our bus.

4. It is not necessary to bring a gift it is your presence that is most desired.

5. She was late for her piano lesson this afternoon it will never happen again.

6. Jeremy's backyard is quite large it is great for running around in.

7. The last city we visited was Stockholm it was my favourite.

8. The Art History test was very difficult Molly and Keith did quite well.

9. The Mona Lisa is in Paris I don't think I will ever see it in person.

10. He had a difficult time with the yard work he will ask for help next time.

D. Write two sentences using the semicolon.

1. _____

2. _____

ISBN: 978-1-897457-05-4

Dashes

The **dash** (−) is yet another form of punctuation used to indicate a pause in a sentence. It is used to insert explanatory material.

Example: Understanding one's limitations − time, ability, and money − makes it easier to make plans in life.

E. Add dashes to the sentences where appropriate.

1. The cities we will visit Rome, Paris, and London will all be very interesting.

2. Teresa was happy to find out the surprise a new puppy!

3. Gavin put on his blue sweater the one his grandmother knitted for him before he went outside.

4. The camp offers a variety of activities soccer, crafts, swimming, photography, and cooking so there is something for every kid to enjoy.

F. Put commas, colons, semicolons, and dashes in the passage.

Ms. Duncan's grade six class went to Kearney for a week-long trip in June. The kids learned a number of things how to canoe how to make dream catchers and how to work in teams. One morning they stopped by a marsh to learn about insects that live in water. "Let's study these insects" Ms. Duncan said. The camp leaders were glad that every kid had brought insect repellent in tubes aerosol cans are not good for the environment. Each evening a leader named Mike would teach the kids a new song one of which was called "The Merry Moose" so the kids could sing their way back to the cabins afterwards.

unit 12 Writing Paragraphs

Paragraphs

A **paragraph** consists of one or more sentences on an idea or topic. A good paragraph often has the following:

topic sentence – the main idea
supporting details – information such as facts and examples
concluding sentence – a summary of the main idea or a solution to a problem

One of the easiest types of paragraphs to write is the **narrative paragraph**. It describes an event or tells a story.

A. Underline the topic sentence, supporting details, or the concluding sentence as indicated for each narrative paragraph.

1. **Topic sentence and concluding sentence**

Today, each child in class had to write a riddle and pass it to the person sitting behind him or her. Marie got Jonathan's riddle and took a very long time to figure it out; the answer was "Marie". Apparently, Jonathan had written a riddle about her, something she would never have expected!

2. **Supporting details**

Natalie fell and hurt herself when she went for a bike ride yesterday. The strap on her left sandal got caught in the pedal and she lost balance. Natalie hurt her knee but luckily, she did not injure her kneecap. She told herself that she would wear her sneakers when riding the bike next time.

ISBN: 978-1-897457-05-4

B. **Write a narrative paragraph on each given topic.**

1. **Title: At School Today**

Topic sentence: _____

_____

Supporting details: _____

_____

_____

_____

Concluding sentence: _____

_____

2. **Title: At Home Today**

Topic sentence: _____

_____

Supporting details: _____

_____

_____

_____

Concluding sentence: _____

_____

ISBN: 978-1-897457-05-4

Descriptive Paragraphs

A **descriptive paragraph** describes something or someone. For example, you can describe your best friend, including details such as what she is like and where she lives.

C. Write a descriptive paragraph on one of the suggested topics.

My Family

My Favourite Game

My Teacher

My Favourite Book

Title: _____

Topic sentence: _____

_____

_____

Supporting details: _____

_____

_____

_____

_____

Concluding sentence: _____

_____

_____

ISBN: 978-1-897457-05-4

Persuasive Paragraphs

A **persuasive paragraph** tries to convince the reader of something. It may start with a phrase such as "I think that...", followed by a support section that includes sentences such as "One reason is..." or "For example..." The concluding sentence may be "This is why I think that..."

D. Write a persuasive paragraph on one of the suggested topics.

Why It Is Good to Read Every Day
Why I Like Playing Music
Why a Dog Is a Kid's Best Friend
Why It Is Good to Exercise Every Day

Title: _____

Topic sentence: _____

_____

Supporting details: _____

_____

_____

_____

_____

_____

_____

Concluding sentence: _____

_____

> **Formal Writing**
>
> A good example of formal writing is the **business letter**. It has a specific purpose and usually contains three paragraphs.
>
> Paragraph 1 – states the purpose of your letter
> Paragraph 2 – gives details of the subject of your letter
> Paragraph 3 – suggests a course of action, offers a solution, or asks for a follow-up

A. Check the situations where writing a business type of letter would be suitable.

1. keeping in contact with an aunt who lives in another province _____

2. suggesting a fundraising idea to the principal _____

3. asking a corporation to be more environmentally conscious _____

4. finding out how a friend is enjoying summer camp _____

5. asking a store if they are hiring part-time staff _____

6. complaining to a newspaper about an article it has published _____

B. Suggest three other situations where one might write a business letter.

1. _____

2. _____

3. _____

C. You have recently purchased a video game. Write a formal letter to the company to tell them how you like or dislike their product.

ISBN: 978-1-897457-05-4

Formal salutation

Dear _____ :

First paragraph

Second paragraph

Third paragraph

Formal closing

Yours truly,

_____

> **Informal Writing**
>
> **Informal writing** does not have to follow precise rules of grammar. The sentence structure can be casual, and contractions are often used. We tend to write informally in postcards, notes, greeting cards, and e-mails.
>
> *Example*: We all went skating at Orkus Skatepark. (formal)
>
> Went skating at Orkus Skatepark. (informal)

D. Rewrite the examples of formal writing to make them informal.

1. Dear Mrs. Benson,

   It was lovely to hear from you earlier this week.

   _____ ,

   _____

2. I am very excited about attending summer camp; I am sure it will be fun.

   _____

   _____

3. If you have any further questions, do not hesitate to contact me.

   _____

E. Rewrite the examples of informal writing to make them formal.

1. Hey Jen! How's it going?

   _____ ,

   _____

2. We'll go skiing later. It'll be totally awesome!

   _____

ISBN: 978-1-897457-05-4

F. Rewrite the following letter into an informal e-mail.

Dear Tina,

My family and I arrived in Montreal on Saturday. I am having a great time here! On Sunday, we all went skating at Orkus Skatepark, the largest indoor skate park in Canada.

Although I have been here for only a few days, I am already talking to my cousins in French. They speak English, too, but I am going to practise my French with them so that I can surprise Madame Le Blanc in the new year.

We will spend two days in Ottawa before coming back to Toronto. I hope all is well with you. I will write again soon.

Sincerely,

Chantal

_____

_____

_____

_____

_____

_____

_____

_____

A. Read the story. Circle the conjunctions.

Mr. and Mrs. Garcia are happy to see Ivan and Marissa use their imaginations. They are glad that the children have forgotten about television and video games. Still, they insist that the children eat their dinner before they leave the table. Ivan and Marissa decide to eat quickly.

Ivan and Marissa cannot wait to study the bottle after they have finished eating. They stay up late in their tent and discuss their ideas of whom it might have belonged to.

"Maybe it belonged to a sailor or maybe even a pirate!" suggests Ivan.

"Maybe a sailor left it here after he saved a princess!" says Marissa.

Ivan shakes the bottle and thinks he hears something. "There is something inside the bottle but I don't know what it is!" he says.

"It could be a clue to whom the bottle belonged unless it is just some sand," says Marissa. "We need something small to go inside the bottle because we won't be able to fit our hands in there," she notes.

The two children are even more interested in solving the mystery so they search very thoroughly. Ivan thinks a twig will do the trick although Marissa is doubtful. Ivan is right and out comes a note!

B. Write "noun", "adjective", or "adverb" on the line to indicate which type of phrase is underlined in each sentence.

1. The note falls out of the shiny bottle and lands on <u>Marissa's sleeping bag</u>.

   _____

2. Marissa picks up the note <u>very quickly</u>.

   _____

3. Ivan takes <u>the brass bottle</u> and places it in his lap.

   _____

4. Ivan's eyes are <u>big and wide</u> as he anxiously waits to hear what the note says.

   _____

5. The note looks <u>old and tattered</u>.

   _____

6. Marissa reads the note <u>clearly and carefully</u>.

   _____

C. Fill in each blank using the suitable infinitive or gerund phrase.

to know the identity	to look for more clues
reading aloud	solving the mystery
to hurry up	to go searching

1. Marissa is very good at _____ because she speaks very clearly.

2. Ivan and Marissa want _____ of the writer.

3. Both of them are very excited about _____ .

4. Ivan wants Marissa _____ because he cannot wait any longer.

5. The note asks for the reader _____ for the writer.

6. They need more information, so they decide that they should search the

   beach _____ .

D. Use the suitable independent and dependent clauses to complete the sentences.

> Marissa gives Ivan the note   they are sure they will find more clues
> after they finish eating their breakfast   he reads the note to himself
> although he already knows what the note says

1. Ivan hands Marissa the brass bottle and _____

   _____ .

2. _____ and thinks about it for a while.

3. _____ ,

   Ivan thinks about it more seriously after reading it himself.

4. In the morning, Ivan and Marissa get ready to leave the campsite _____

   _____ .

5. _____ and that

   this new information they find will solve the mystery by the end of the day.

E. Write "adj" or "adv" to indicate whether the underlined clauses are adjectival or adverbial.

1. Ivan and Marissa gather their belongings <u>before they leave the campsite</u>.   _____

2. The bottle, <u>which is a bit heavy</u>, is difficult to carry.   _____

3. They decide to look around <u>where they found the bottle</u>.   _____

4. <u>After they see there is nothing there</u>, they decide to move on.   _____

ISBN: 978-1-897457-05-4

F. **Read the passage. Then write "simple", "compound", or "complex"
to indicate which type of sentence is underlined.**

Ivan and Marissa continue to walk along the beach. <u>They walk quickly.</u>
(1.   ) Ivan hopes to find a pirate's treasure. <u>They are just about
to give up when they see some movement up ahead.</u> (2.   ) As
they get closer, they can see some children digging in the sand. "Maybe they
have already found where the pirate's treasure is!" says Ivan.

Ivan and Marissa approach the children to see what they are doing. <u>A girl
is crying.</u> (3.   ) They learn that her name is Tammy. "What is the
matter?" Marissa asks Tammy.

"<u>I've lost something!</u>" (4.   ) says Tammy.

"Is it buried treasure?" asks Ivan.

"No. <u>It is my grandmother's brass bottle and I can't find it anywhere!</u>"
(5.   ) she cries.

<u>Ivan and Marissa realize the bottle they have belongs to Tammy so they
hand it to her.</u> (6.   ) "We found your bottle yesterday. We didn't
know it belonged to anyone," says Ivan. <u>Tammy stops crying after she hears
this.</u> (7.   ) She turns to her friends to show them. <u>Ivan and Marissa
are disappointed to see the
bottle go but they know they
did the right thing.</u>
(8.   )

"I guess we won't have
any more fun," says Ivan as
they walk away.

G. Add commas, colons, semicolons, and dashes to the passage where appropriate.

"I just remembered the note!" says Marissa. Ivan and Marissa race back to where they met Tammy. "We forgot to tell you" says Marissa "we found something inside the bottle an old note that must belong to your grandmother!" Ivan hands Tammy the note.

"Actually my friend Carlos wrote that note" Tammy says pointing to the boy standing next to her. "Sorry to disappoint you but we were just playing."

"We thought it might have belonged to a sailor or a pirate!" says Ivan.

"We were playing something like that" Tammy says. "Would you like to play with us?" Ivan and Marissa are happy she has asked they decide to stay and play.

H. Underline the topic sentence and concluding sentence of the following narrative paragraph.

Ivan and Marissa play with Tammy, Carlos, and the other children for the rest of their camping trip. They play some games that involve the bottle. One of these games is pretending they are sailors lost at sea who are sending messages in bottles. They play other games, too. Ivan and Marissa have lots of fun and are sad to leave when the trip is over. They have discovered that using their imagination can be a lot more fun than playing computer and video games.

ISBN: 978-1-897457-05-4

I. Rewrite the formal letter into an informal letter.

Dear Tammy:

It was wonderful to meet you, Carlos, and all of your friends this summer at Sandbanks Provincial Park. We had a fabulous time playing games with you on the beach.

We have arrived home safely and will begin school in a few weeks. Our favourite subjects are History and Science. Which subjects are you looking forward to?

Until school starts, we will continue to play the sailor game we played with you at the park. We hope you can visit us one day so that you can join us.

Sincerely,

Ivan and Marissa

_____

_____

_____

_____

_____

_____

_____

_____

_____

ISBN: 978-1-897457-05-4

Grammar Summary

Nouns

A **noun** names a person, an animal, a place, or a thing. It can be a **countable common noun**, an **uncountable common noun**, a **proper noun**, or a **compound proper noun**.

A noun can be the **object** of a verb in a sentence. There are two types of objects: direct objects and indirect objects.

A **direct object** is the receiver of the action of the verb.

An **indirect object** is to whom or what the action of the verb is directed.

Pronouns

A **pronoun** replaces a noun in a sentence. There are different types of pronouns:

A **subject pronoun** takes the place of the subject noun.

An **object pronoun** takes the place of the object noun.

A **reflexive pronoun** is a type of object pronoun. It is used when the subject's action turns back on the subject.

A **demonstrative pronoun** identifies people or points to physical objects.

A **relative pronoun** relates to a previously occurring noun in the sentence.

Modal Verbs

Modal verbs like "can" and "could" are used with verbs to talk about ability, permission, and possibility.

To ask for assistance in a polite way, "will", "would", or "could" can be used.

Verb Tenses

The **simple present tense** is used to talk about a habit or a simple truth.

The **present progressive tense** is used to talk about an action that is going on, or an action that will take place in the near future.

The **simple past tense** is used to talk about something that happened habitually or at a particular time in the past.

ISBN: 978-1-897457-05-4

The **past progressive tense** is used to talk about something that continued to happen over a period of time in the past.

The **simple future tense** is used to talk about something that will happen.

The **future progressive tense** is used to talk about something that will happen over a period of time.

Voices

The **active voice** is used when we want to talk about a person or thing doing something.

The **passive voice** is used when we want to focus on the person or thing affected by something. We often do not mention the one that performs the action.

Adjectives and Adverbs

Comparative adjectives and **comparative adverbs** compare two people, animals, things, or groups.

Superlative adjectives and **superlative adverbs** compare three or more people, animals, things, or groups.

Some verbs can become adjectives when "ing" or "ed" is added to them.

Examples

- Johnny asks Darla if she can mail the letters for him.

  Johnny – proper noun

  asks – simple present tense verb

  Darla – proper noun; direct object

  she – subject pronoun referring to Darla

  can – modal verb used with the verb "mail" to show possibility

  the letters – countable common noun; direct object

  him – object pronoun referring to Johnny

- Darla was asked because she is the most responsible of all Johnny's friends.

  Darla was asked – passive voice

  most responsible – superlative adjective

Conjunctions

A **conjunction** is a word that joins together words, phrases, or sentences.

Some conjunctions like "either...or", "neither...nor", and "not only...but also" are used in pairs.

Phrases

A **noun phrase** functions like a noun in a sentence. It can be the subject, object, or the complement.

An **adjective phrase** functions like an adjective in a sentence. It describes a noun.

An **adverb phrase** functions like an adverb. It describes a verb.

An **infinitive phrase** contains a verb that follows "to".

A **gerund phrase** contains a verb in the "ing" form. It can function as the subject, object, complement, or the object of preposition in a sentence.

Clauses

An **independent clause** can function as a complete sentence.

A **dependent clause** cannot function as a complete sentence. It needs an independent clause to make its meaning complete.

An **adjectival clause** gives information about a noun in a sentence.

An **adverbial clause** tells where or when the action of a verb takes place.

Sentences

A **simple sentence** is formed whenever there is a subject and a verb.

A **compound sentence** has two or more independent clauses.

A **complex sentence** has an independent clause and one or more dependent clauses.

ISBN: 978-1-897457-05-4

Punctuation

The **comma** (**,**) indicates one or more pauses in a sentence.

The **colon** (**:**) indicates pauses, joins two sentences when the second explains the first, or sets off a concluding statement. It can also be used to introduce a list of items.

The **semicolon** (**;**) indicates pauses or joins two separate sentences when the second elaborates on the first. It can also be used to replace conjunctions.

The **dash** (**–**) is used to indicate a pause or insert explanatory material.

Paragraphs

A **paragraph** consists of one or more sentences on an idea or topic. A good paragraph often has a topic sentence, supporting details, and a concluding sentence.

A **narrative paragraph** describes an event or tells a story.

A **descriptive paragraph** describes something or someone.

A **persuasive paragraph** tries to convince the reader of something.

Formal and Informal Writing

Formal writing has a specific purpose and follows the rules of grammar.

Informal writing does not have to follow precise rules of grammar. The sentence structure can be casual, and contractions are often used.

Example

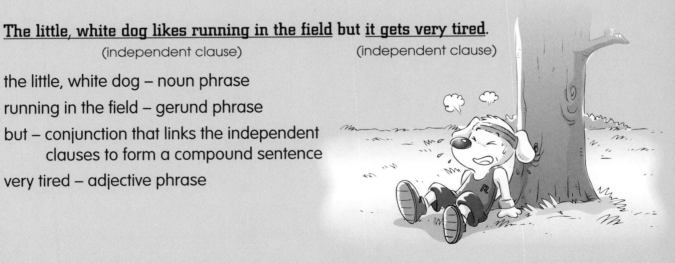

- <u>The little, white dog likes running in the field</u> but <u>it gets very tired</u>.
  (independent clause)   (independent clause)

  the little, white dog – noun phrase

  running in the field – gerund phrase

  but – conjunction that links the independent clauses to form a compound sentence

  very tired – adjective phrase

ISBN: 978-1-897457-05-4

We are cheery birds.

cheery

DICTIONARY

ISBN: 978-1-897457-05-4

1 The Topic Sentence

A **topic sentence** introduces the main idea of a paragraph. Topic sentences must be focused enough to let the reader know what the paragraph is about.

A. Circle the letter of the most appropriate topic sentence from each group below.

Base your selection on the following criteria:
a. creates interest for the reader
b. gives sufficient information or direction as to what is being written about
c. gives a more focused topic

1 The Storm

A. It was a stormy night.

B. Dark clouds covered the sky.

C. When we saw the storm coming, we made the necessary preparations to protect ourselves.

2 The Final Game

A. The score in the final game was close.

B. With the score tied and minutes left to play in the final game, the unthinkable happened.

C. No one was ready for what happened during the final game.

3 The New Family Pet

A. Our friends and neighbours were shocked when they first saw the new family pet we brought home.

B. Every family should have a new pet every now and then.

C. Some animals make ideal family pets.

4 The Greatest Show on Earth

A. The Cirque du Soleil provided the greatest night of entertainment our family had ever experienced.

B. Everyone enjoys the circus.

C. Our family went to the circus for the first time.

ISBN: 978-1-897457-05-4

Composing Topic Sentences

B. Compose an interesting and informative topic sentence for each paragraph below. Add a title for each paragraph.

≡ Paragraph 1 ≡   Title: _____

Topic Sentence: _____

_____ .

The hotel we stayed at was located right on the beach. Every day after breakfast, we would cool off in the clear, warm water of the Atlantic. In the afternoons, we often played tennis on the courts next to the hotel or miniature golf at the play centre across the road. Everyone was so pleased with the holiday that we decided to return next year.

≡ Paragraph 2 ≡   Title: _____

Topic Sentence: _____

_____ .

Just before the race was to begin, our best runner, Lauren, got a cramp in her side. She was doubled up in pain and was unable to compete. Our hopes of winning the 200-metre race disappeared. Suddenly, she stood up and, despite the discomfort of the cramp, declared that she would compete. The whole school cheered when she stepped up to the starting line.

≡ Paragraph 3 ≡   Title: _____

Topic Sentence: _____

_____ .

Once the seat was adjusted and he took a few practice turns with the bike, he was ready for a long ride. The eighteen speeds made climbing hills easy. He rode along the lake road, through the woods, and along the bike path next to the highway. He stopped at the roadside to eat a sandwich he had packed and to take a drink of water. After riding for an hour, he turned and headed back for home. In total, he had ridden 50 kilometres on the new bike. He knew that with this bike, he could plan many more bike-riding adventures.

ISBN: 978-1-897457-05-4

Composing Paragraphs

C. **Below are topic sentences. Compose a short paragraph of three or four sentences for each topic.**

1. Camping is a wonderful way to experience nature particularly if your campsite is deep in the wilderness. _____

   _____

   _____

   _____

   _____

   _____

   _____

2. Richard and Paul were very excited about going into grade six because they would be moving into the new building equipped with lockers and a new gymnasium. _____

   _____

   _____

   _____

   _____

   _____

   _____

3. To make this picnic memorable, the group decided to pack their favourite foods including some irresistible snacks. _____

   _____

   _____

   _____

   _____

   _____

   _____

> *Weak topic sentences can be improved by adding more information.*

Example: Topic sentence: Building sand sculptures is fun.

Improved topic sentence: With a shovel, a bucket, and a little imagination, there is no limit to what sand sculptures you can create.

D. Improve the following topic sentences.

1. The movie was scary.

   Improved topic sentence: _____

   _____

   _____

2. My cousins arrived today from Italy.

   Improved topic sentence: _____

   _____

3. The sky went black.

   Improved topic sentence: _____

   _____

   _____

4. Today was our moving day.

   Improved topic sentence: _____

   _____

5. Today we were having a science test.

   Improved topic sentence: _____

   _____

   _____

6. We learned an important lesson that day.

   Improved topic sentence: _____

   _____

2 Following the Topic Sentence

A. For each topic sentence below, add two or three more sentences to make a complete paragraph. The sentences you create should further develop the topic sentence.

1. In the middle of the night, I heard a strange noise outside my bedroom window.

_____

_____

_____

_____

_____

_____

2. The pilot announced over the speaker that we should fasten our seatbelts because we were in for a rough landing.

_____

_____

_____

_____

_____

_____

_____

3. The package addressed to me was delivered by courier, and when I opened it, I was shocked.

_____

_____

_____

_____

_____

_____

   ISBN: 978-1-897457-05-4

Creating Paragraphs

B. Create a paragraph of three or four sentences using as many words in each group as possible.

> A **paragraph** is a group of sentences that are closely related in topic.

moon   trees   campsite   bears

wind   noises   fire   twigs   scary

campfire   tent   lantern   breakfast

leader   stars   sleeping   stories   woods

leaves   sleeping bags   snoring   laughter

marshmallows   porridge   darkness

Title: _____

_____

_____

_____

_____

_____

_____

_____

_____

_____

_____

ISBN: 978-1-897457-05-4

party	friends	surprise	balloons	cake	afternoon
ice cream	gifts			hiding	lights
darkness	candles			funny	games
singing	music			parents	winners
home	food			spilled	cards
Saturday	bowling			strike	noisy

Title: _____

_____

_____

_____

_____

_____

_____

_____

_____

_____

_____

C. **Write a topic sentence for each short paragraph below. The topic sentence should introduce the main idea of the paragraph.**

1. _____

_____

We had never been on a cruise ship before and we were very excited. When the ship blasted its horn and pulled away, we stood on the deck and waved at the people on the pier even though we didn't know them. We were on our way to visit six Caribbean islands in seven days at sea.

ISBN: 978-1-897457-05-4

2. _____

_____

The line up for rides were long and it was very hot outside. Luckily, we had brought bottles of water with us. Finally, it was our turn to board the ride and each one of us was scared stiff.

3. _____

_____

He approached the free throw line and bounced the ball a few times to set himself. The crowd behind the basket tried to distract him but he concentrated on the rim. The ball went up rotating in the air. It landed on the rim, bounced, spun, wavered, wobbled, and finally fell through the hoop.

4. _____

_____

The puppy ran around the house, sliding on the hardwood floors and bumping into the dining room chairs. He ran under the table and began tugging on the loose table cloth. Training this little monster was going to be a big job.

5. _____

_____

The trainer showed us a number of horses and asked us to choose the one we would like to ride. After we got in the saddle, our guide began leading us in a slow trot. Then, we broke into a mild gallop and suddenly horseback riding became thrilling.

ISBN: 978-1-897457-05-4

3 Descriptive Language (1)

To make your writing more interesting and meaningful, try using more descriptive words for the things you are writing about. Some words are more descriptive than others although they may have similar meaning.

A. For each sentence, underline the most appropriate word to replace the italicized word.

1. They rested in the ski *building*.

   lodge   home   tower   apartment

2. The *big house* had twelve bedrooms and three living rooms.

   chalet   mansion   residence   dwelling

3. The *loud* dog growled at the postman.

   careful   ferocious   rude   unhappy

4. She read a *good* book.

   interesting   thick   short   long

5. They laughed at the *man who told jokes on stage*.

   actor   entertainer   comedian   singer

6. The *tall* boy played basketball.

   thin   slight   lofty   lanky

7. He bought a shiny, new, red *vehicle*.

   car   automobile   convertible   auto

8. The *building* flashed a light to warn sailors.

   tower   structure   lighthouse   skyscraper

9. The *athlete* prepared for the race.

   professional   sprinter   runner   jogger

10. They enjoyed a *nice* meal at the new restaurant.

    hot   unusual   juicy   gourmet

ISBN: 978-1-897457-05-4

Action Verbs

Use an action verb to give the reader a better understanding of what is actually happening in the sentence. Consider the context of each sentence.

Example: 1. He <u>went</u> down the ice towards the net.
2. He **roared** down the ice towards the net.

B. From the list of verbs below each sentence, underline the best replacement for the italicized verb.

1. He *walked* down the street slowly.

    sauntered   ran   hopped   glided

2. They *went* home to get money before the show started.

    strolled   rushed   drifted   arrived

3. The dog *jumped up* in the air to catch the Frisbee.

    leaped   rose   bounced   elevated

4. The bird *came* down out of the sky to catch the fish.

    dropped   flew   swooped   slipped

5. He *skated* around the defensemen and scored a goal.

    circled   zigzagged   squeezed   slid

6. The door *shut* from a sudden gust of wind through the house.

    closed   locked   swung   slammed

7. The sailboat *moved* lazily in the breeze.

    drifted   sailed   roared   travelled

8. Lightning *was seen* across the black sky.

    slashed   screamed   flashed   sparked

9. The sun *shone* down on the sunbathers on the beach.

    lit   sprayed   touched   blazed

10. The lion *ate* the huge hunks of raw meat.

    consumed   devoured   had   enjoyed

Understanding Meaning through Context

C. **Match the underlined words with the meanings listed below. Use the context to determine the meaning of the underlined words.**

The <u>sleek</u> sailboat <u>floated</u> <u>gingerly</u> across the <u>undulating</u> water. The bright sails billowed in the breeze as the bow dipped <u>gracefully</u> in and out of the waves. A <u>refreshing</u> spray of water splashed upon the slippery deck.

The captain announced a warning to the crew, cautioning them about the <u>precarious</u> condition of the wet deck. Suddenly, one of the crew <u>shrieked</u> before <u>careening</u> backwards into the lake. The captain <u>roared</u>, "Man overboard!" <u>Efficiently</u> the crew <u>executed</u> an <u>instantaneous</u> rescue. The <u>voyage</u> continued without further <u>complications</u>.

1. immediate   _____

2. carefully, cautiously   _____

3. spoke loudly, yelled   _____

4. trip, tour   _____

5. dangerous, threatening   _____

6. cool, fresh   _____

7. slim, narrow, streamlined   _____

8. performed, made happen   _____

9. difficulties, problems   _____

10. curving, wavy   _____

11. performed with skill, expertly   _____

12. bobbed, drifted, stayed above water   _____

13. gently, easily, smoothly, with control   _____

14. leaning, tilting   _____

15. screamed, screeched, howled   _____

Creating Adjectives from Verbs

A **participle** is an adjective form of a verb.

Example: verb – walk
adjective form – walking
The old man used a **walking** stick for balance.

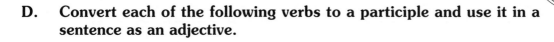

D. Convert each of the following verbs to a participle and use it in a sentence as an adjective.

1. sing
_____

2. dine
_____

3. run
_____

4. cry
_____

5. speak
_____

6. fish
_____

7. swim
_____

8. drive
_____

9. burn
_____

10. fall
_____

4 Confusing Words

 Frequently Misspelled Words

A. Circle the correct spelling from the choices for each of these frequently misspelled words.

If you are unsure, use your dictionary.

1.	noticeable	noticeble	noticable
2.	defenite	definate	definite
3.	sucess	success	succes
4.	heros	heroes	heross
5.	occurrence	ocurrence	occurence
6.	neccessary	necesary	necessary
7.	receive	recive	recieve
8.	therefor	therefour	therefore
9.	professer	profesor	professor
10.	arguement	argument	argament

 Working with Homonyms

Homonyms are words that sound alike but have different meanings.

Examples: "whether" and "weather"

He asked **whether** or not I was going to school today because the **weather** forecast called for a storm.

B. Circle the correct word to suit the meaning (context) of each sentence below.

1. They waited for there / their ride home after school.

2. She received many presence / presents for her birthday.

ISBN: 978-1-897457-05-4

3. The dog dug a hole / whole in which to bury its bone.

4. She was very sad when her fish past / passed away.

5. " Whose / Who's in charge?" she inquired.

6. The ship sailed out of site / sight into the sunset.

7. Because he hadn't eaten, he felt week / weak .

8. The enemies fought a duel / dual with swords.

9. She came forth / fourth in the 100-metre sprint.

10. The wobbly bicycle wheel was loose / lose .

11. The tailor will alter / altar his suit.

12. The campers worried about a bear / bare in the woods.

13. He had a heavy load to bear / bare .

14. The herd / heard of elephants stopped by the river for a drink.

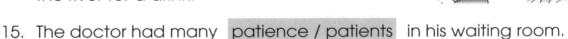

15. The doctor had many patience / patients in his waiting room.

16. The principle / principal of the school visited the classrooms.

17. The plane / plain was forced to land on the open plane / plain .

18. The council / counsel will give council / counsel to the recruits.

19. Because he had a cold, his voice was hoarse / horse .

20. She wrote in her dairy / diary the events of her holiday.

21. They paid their fare / fair to go to the fare / fair .

22. She took a coffee break / brake in the morning only.

23. The soldiers were there to keep the peace / piece .

24. Geography was his favourite school coarse / course .

25. They were bored / board with the movie they were watching.

Tricky Usage Problems

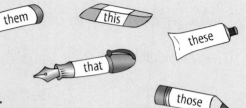

this   that   them   these   those

"This" and "that" modify single nouns.

"Them", "these", and "those" modify plural nouns.

Note 1:   "Those" may be either an adjective or a pronoun.
"Them" is always a pronoun and never an adjective.

Note 2:   Words such as "type of", "sort of", and "kind of" are treated as singular.

C.   Circle the correct word for each sentence.

1.   She chose   this / these   sort of book to read on the train.

2.   He put   these / them   clothes in the dresser.

3.   This / Them   type of game is very challenging.

4.   That / Those   types of people are fun to be with.

5.   She preferred to sing   this / those   kind of song.

6.   He is happy with   that / these   types of activity.

7.   This / Those   kinds of sports are dangerous.

8.   She called   them / those   on the telephone.

9.   Those / That   kind of pizza was his favourite.

More Tricky Usage

good   bad   badly   well

"Good" should be used only as an adjective.

Example: He had a **good** time at the party.
Incorrect: She did not feel **good**.
Correct: She did not feel **well**.

"Bad" is used after a linking verb.

Example: She felt **bad** about missing the rehearsal.

"Badly" is used after an action verb.

Example: He played **badly** in the final game.

"Well" is used after an action verb.

Example: He played **well** in the final game.
Incorrect: He played **good** in the final game.

   ISBN: 978-1-897457-05-4

D. Write the correct word in the space provided.

1. The coach felt _____ about the team's victory.

good / well

2. The food tastes _____ because it was not refrigerated.

bad / badly

3. She was _____ at being a soccer goalkeeper.

good / well

4. He felt _____ about the news that he was moving away.

bad / badly

5. She sang _____ because she had a sore throat.

bad / badly

6. He felt _____ after a long rest in bed.

good / well

"Fewer" and "Less"

"Fewer" refers to an exact number; "less" refers to an amount or quantity.

Incorrect:	There were **less** people in the audience.
Correct:	There were **fewer** people in the audience
Incorrect:	He drank **less** bottles of water than he needed.
Correct:	He drank **fewer** bottles of water than he needed.

E. Circle the correct term for each sentence.

1. She had written (fewer / less) words in her story than required.

2. He drank (fewer / less) milk than he did when he was younger.

3. (Less / Fewer) people are taking public transit than predicted.

4. There were (fewer / less) cases of influenza this past winter.

5. As the expression goes: (less / fewer) is more.

6. The teacher had (less / fewer) concerns because the students all did well.

5 · Creating a Story Ending

A story is often made up of a conflict or a situation that needs to be solved. A story ending is the part of the story where the problem or conflict is finally solved. Often, suspense or a series of events is used to build towards a story ending.

A. Below is a story about a track and field event. Provide an ending paragraph for the story in the space provided. Add a title that suits your ending.

Title: _____

The mid-June day of the final track and field meet was met by temperatures approaching 30°C. The air was still and the scorching sun blazed down on the competitors who huddled under the sparse trees for shade. Litres of water were being consumed by the athletes before competing. Some just poured the water over their heads in a vain attempt at momentary relief.

Lisa, an 11-year-old sprinter, was the one hope her school had of bringing home a ribbon. She specialized in the 200-metre race, a race that demanded endurance and strategy. Small in size, she was big in heart, and her legs were like pistons pumping fiercely when she ran. Lisa had placed first in the divisional race and second in the regional where she was defeated by a mere 2 seconds by her main competitor, another 11-year-old runner named Jennifer. Jennifer was a tall girl with long legs that enabled her to run in steady, loping strides. Both runners were fierce competitors and superb athletes. Both were determined to win.

The announcement came for the 200-metre final – runners were asked to report to the starter. There was a swell of spectators gathering at the finish line anticipating a spectacular finish. Lisa and Jennifer set themselves into the starting blocks staring straight ahead. They arched their backs and lowered their heads. The starter raised the pistol, and at the sound of the shot, they were off – the championship race was on.

30 metres into the race, Lisa and Jennifer, neck and neck, had jumped out to an insurmountable lead over the other runners. The rest of the field were now

racing for third place as they watched the pair of runners round the first turn and speed down the straight-way. The crowd cheered wildly. At the 100-metre mark, Lisa had taken a slight lead but Jennifer stayed just off her right shoulder waiting to make her move.

At 160 metres, the runners were again neck and neck, well ahead of the pack. Then the unthinkable happened. Lisa soared into the lead, but as she sprinted ahead, she stumbled and sprawled to the ground. The crowd was silenced.

_____

_____

_____

_____

_____

_____

_____

_____

_____

_____

_____

_____

The Parts of a Story

Setting

The setting of a story refers to the time and place in which the story takes place.

B.   State two facts about the setting that are known to the reader immediately.

1.   _____

2.   _____

Characters

Characters in a story can be divided into two basic categories:

(a) **Major characters:** They are usually directly involved in the action or conflict.

(b) **Minor characters:** They have limited involvement in the story; sometimes they deliver messages or interact with the major characters to help move the story along.

C.   Who are the major and minor characters in this story?

Major: _____

Minor: _____

Descriptions

A writer will use descriptions to help the reader visualize the setting, the characters, and the action in the story.

D.   State four descriptions that you think are effective.

1.   _____

2.   _____

3.   _____

4.   _____

Plot

Plot refers to the main action that takes place in the story. The plot usually follows a path of development from beginning to end.

E. **Describe the plot of this story.**

_____

_____

_____

Conflict

Conflict often forms the basis of a story. It may involve two persons against each other, a character fighting against himself/herself (decision making), or a character facing nature.

F. **State the central conflict in this story.**

_____

_____

_____

Suspense

Suspense is a technique of writing that "suspends" the reader by holding back information or by giving only partial information to build the ending.

G. **Describe the suspense in this story.**

_____

_____

_____

H. **Is the suspense effective? Explain why or why not.**

_____

_____

_____

6 Word-Building Challenge

Your vocabulary can be expanded by developing new words from a root word.

A. Build a series of words from the root word given (Try adding a prefix or suffix). Then circle the best synonym from the choices given.

A new synonym to add to your vocabulary is given with each question below.

Example:

decide (verb)	Words developed:	decision	decisive
Synonym:	(choose) review	think	list
New synonym:	*resolve* (to solve an issue)		

1. **engage** _____ _____

   Synonym: trap   fix   occupy   engulf

   New synonym: *monopolize* (to control, engage fully)

2. **occur** _____ _____

   Synonym: complete   happen   try   effect

   New synonym: *transpire* (to take place)

3. **rage** _____ _____

   Synonym: feelings   attitude   hate   fury

   New synonym: *fad* (something that becomes popular)

4. **produce** _____ _____

   Synonym: make   repair   apply   destroy

   New synonym: *yield* (to produce as in crops)

ISBN: 978-1-897457-05-4

5.	**neglect**	_____ _____
	Synonym:	hide disappear ignore refuse
	New synonym:	*omit* (to leave out)

6.	**identity**	_____ _____
	Synonym	self search dental imagine
	New synonym:	*individuality* (personal characteristics that set a person apart from others)

B. **Place each new word in the sentence below that suits its meaning.**

monopolize   transpire   fad
yield   omit   individuality

1. The hula-hoop _____ took place in the 1960's.

2. We must be proud of our _____ because it is who we are.

3. If you _____ too many answers on the test, you may not pass.

4. They will wait to see what will _____ over the next few days before they make a decision.

5. The farmer was happy with the _____ from the farm this year.

6. He always tries to _____ the conversation by talking too much.

New Words in Context

C. Circle a suitable synonym for the underlined word in each sentence below.

> *These words may be new to you. Use the meaning (context) of the sentence to help you define the words.*

1. The pain in his knee was <u>tolerable</u> so he was able to continue to run.

    bearable   painful   slight   severe

2. It was a <u>momentous</u> occasion when he received the Most Valuable Player Award.

    useless   boring   important   critical

3. The <u>incompetent</u> driver caused the accident.

    skilled   equipped   incapable   tricky

4. The <u>repulsive</u> monster in the horror movie frightened the audience.

    huge   disgusting   aggressive   sleepy

5. The <u>prominent</u> citizen was popular with the residents of the town.

    dangerous   happy   serious   well-known

6. The <u>obstinate</u> student refused to admit his answer was wrong even though there was proof.

    stubborn   intelligent   careful   sneaky

7. The <u>laborious</u> task of digging the trench tired out even the young workers.

    simple   interesting   difficult   creative

8. It was <u>hazardous</u> driving through the storm at night.

    easy   uneventful   dangerous   amusing

9. He had an <u>extraordinary</u> experience watching the whales off the Gaspé Peninsula.

    boring   frightful   incredible   useful

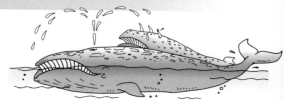

10. The injured animal was a <u>pathetic</u> sight.

    unusual   pitiful   strange   powerful

D. **Write the homonyms using the clues.**

A **homonym** is a word that sounds the same as another word but has a different meaning.

1. (a) look at

st _____

(b) climb one at a time

st _____

2. (a) centre of apple

co _____

(b) army troops

co _____

3. (a) holes in skin

po _____

(b) dispenses a liquid

po _____

4. (a) to come apart

br _____

(b) to stop

br _____

5. (a) bright colour

r _____

(b) book activity

r _____

6. (a) end of day

n _____

(b) in King Arthur's Court

k _____

7. (a) to be permitted

al _____

(b) to speak so all can hear

al _____

8. (a) falls from clouds

r _____

(b) a king's rule

r _____

9. (a) direction to go

w _____

(b) measure heaviness

w _____

10. (a) float on water

sa _____

(b) reduced price

sa _____

 ISBN: 978-1-897457-05-4

7 Descriptive Language (2)

 Descriptive language helps the reader establish a clear picture of what you are describing. In creative writing, it is important to choose words that are precise and colourful.

A. Circle the descriptive word below each sentence that would be a suitable replacement for the italicized word. Choose the one that best fits the context of the sentence.

1. The *awful* road conditions made driving impossible.

   hazardous   smooth   bumpy   tight

2. The students were *happy* that their team won the final game.

   concerned   upset   glad   excited

3. Their new house was so *big* that they had to buy more furniture.

   wide   high   spacious   cramped

4. The creature in the film was so *awful* they couldn't face the screen.

   large   hideous   clever   enormous

5. The homework was so *terrible* that few students completed the work.

   entertaining   challenging   important   necessary

6. At the zoo, they watched the tiger *walk* back and forth in its cage.

   stroll   scamper   skip   pace

7. The noise from the musical instruments was *loud* for the people sitting close to the stage.

   deafening   enjoyable   clear   smooth

8. The surfers *went* over the waves with amazing balance.

   splashed   sunk   glided   dropped

9. The outfielder *moved* to his left to make an unbelievable catch.

   leaned   reached   dove   skipped

ISBN: 978-1-897457-05-4

Words in Context

The meaning of a word can often be figured out by the context (meaning) of a sentence.

B. Read the paragraph below and match each underlined word with a synonym from the list. Use the context to help you decide which words match up.

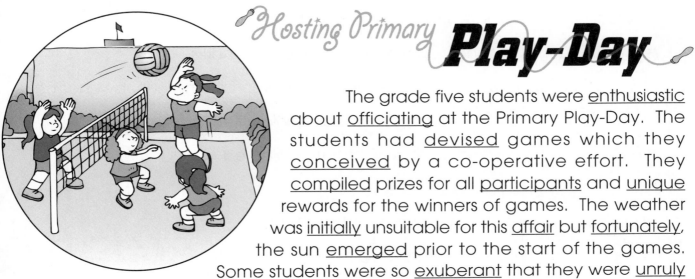

Hosting Primary **Play-Day**

The grade five students were <u>enthusiastic</u> about <u>officiating</u> at the Primary Play-Day. The students had <u>devised</u> games which they <u>conceived</u> by a co-operative effort. They <u>compiled</u> prizes for all <u>participants</u> and <u>unique</u> rewards for the winners of games. The weather was <u>initially</u> unsuitable for this <u>affair</u> but <u>fortunately</u>, the sun <u>emerged</u> prior to the start of the games. Some students were so <u>exuberant</u> that they were <u>unruly</u> at times but when the games began, they <u>composed</u> themselves. The teachers <u>commented</u> that the day was an <u>enormous</u> success.

1. enthusiastic _____
2. officiating _____
3. devised _____
4. conceived _____
5. compiled _____
6. participants _____
7. unique _____
8. initially _____
9. affair _____
10. fortunately _____
11. emerged _____
12. exuberant _____
13. unruly _____
14. composed _____
15. commented _____
16. enormous _____

A.	unusual	B.	huge
C.	players	D.	luckily
E.	came out	F.	at first
G.	excited	H.	misbehaving
I.	controlled	J.	stated
K.	keen	L.	managing
M.	created	N.	planned
O.	collected	P.	event

C. Based on the definitions and synonyms given, place each word in the sentence that best suits its meaning.

grimace .... facial expression of pain

obscure .... difficult to see or find, cloudy

intrigued .... attracted to, interested in, fascinated by

jeering .... mocking, taunting, making rude remarks

coincidental .... happening at the same time as something else, by chance

obstinate .... stubborn, strong-minded, opinionated, firm

ornate .... decorative, showy, brightly coloured

bleak .... dreary, dull, bare

absurd .... ridiculous, unbelievable, unlikely

consecutive ..... in an order or sequence

energetic .... lively, healthy, robust

abundance ..... large quantity of, many of

cantankerous .. grouchy, mean

grievance .... complaint, objection

logical .... analytical, reasonable, proper by choice

Enter the most obvious words first; check each word as you use it.

1. Because there was an _____ of food, everyone had lots to eat.

2. The fans who were _____ the losing team were asked to leave the arena.

3. The morning weather looked _____ until the clouds lifted.

ISBN: 978-1-897457-05-4

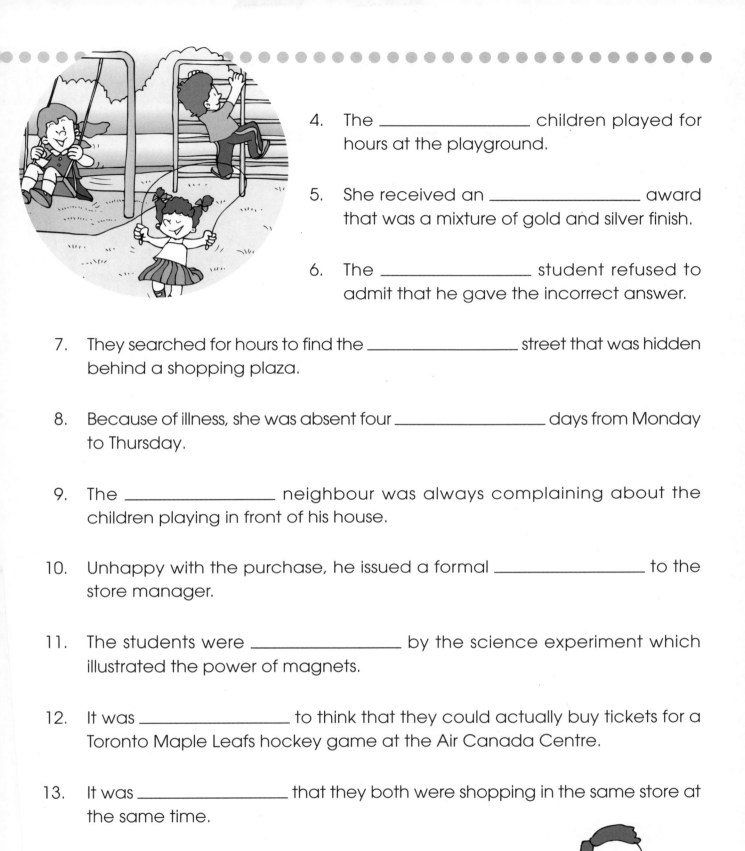

4.   The _____ children played for hours at the playground.

5.   She received an _____ award that was a mixture of gold and silver finish.

6.   The _____ student refused to admit that he gave the incorrect answer.

7.   They searched for hours to find the _____ street that was hidden behind a shopping plaza.

8.   Because of illness, she was absent four _____ days from Monday to Thursday.

9.   The _____ neighbour was always complaining about the children playing in front of his house.

10. Unhappy with the purchase, he issued a formal _____ to the store manager.

11. The students were _____ by the science experiment which illustrated the power of magnets.

12. It was _____ to think that they could actually buy tickets for a Toronto Maple Leafs hockey game at the Air Canada Centre.

13. It was _____ that they both were shopping in the same store at the same time.

14. The _____ on his face showed his exhaustion after the race.

15. The _____ answer was the one that appeared reasonable at first thought.

A. Circle the best topic sentence from each group of sentences below.

1 The Party

A. We went to a birthday party.

B. We went to a birthday party for Susan.

C. Susan's surprise birthday party was planned in secret by her best friend, Lara.

2 Relatives

A. The first time he met his relatives from Italy was when they arrived in Calgary to attend his sister's wedding.

B. Relatives love coming to weddings.

C. Always invite all your relatives to a wedding.

3 Raccoons

A. Raccoons love eating garbage.

B. Hungry raccoons are very clever at opening even the most secure garbage containers.

C. No garbage container can stop a raccoon.

4 The Library

A. Libraries are not just a place to get books.

B. The library is an ideal place to do your homework because there are many resources to use and it is quiet there.

C. If you have a homework assignment, go to the library.

5 Exercise

A. Exercise is important for staying healthy.

B. Regular exercise is good for people of all ages but we should never overdo it.

C. Children, not just adults, should exercise regularly to maintain their health.

ISBN: 978-1-897457-05-4

B. **Match each of the words or phrases below with its more descriptive form.**

1. building at a ski resort _____
2. large house _____
3. dangerous _____
4. good book _____
5. funny performer _____
6. tall _____
7. vehicle _____
8. downtown building _____
9. athlete _____
10. nice meal _____

A. Ferrari
B. mystery novel
C. comedian
D. lanky
E. gourmet delight
F. sprinter
G. ferocious
H. chalet
I. mansion
J. skyscraper

C. **Match the dull, uninteresting verbs on the left with the more vivid synonyms on the right.**

1. walked (person) _____
2. went in a hurry (person) _____
3. jumped up (animal) _____
4. came down (bird) _____
5. skated (person) _____
6. shut (door) _____
7. moved (sailboat) _____
8. was seen (lightning) _____
9. shone (sun) _____
10. ate (animal) _____

A. devoured
B. swooped
C. zigzagged
D. glided
E. flashed
F. sauntered
G. rushed
H. slammed
I. leaped
J. blazed

D. Match each of the words with its meaning.

GROUP ONE

1. immediate _____
2. carefully _____
3. yelled _____
4. tour _____
5. dangerous _____

A. roared
B. voyage
C. precarious
D. gingerly
E. instantaneous

GROUP TWO

6. cool, fresh _____
7. streamlined _____
8. performed _____
9. difficulties _____
10. wavy _____

A. undulating
B. refreshing
C. complications
D. sleek
E. executed

GROUP THREE

11. skilfully _____
12. bobbed _____
13. smoothly _____
14. tilting _____
15. screamed _____

A. careening
B. shrieked
C. floated
D. gracefully
E. efficiently

E. Mark each word as spelled correctly (C) or incorrectly (I). Add the corrected version.

1. noticable _____ _____
2. argument _____ _____
3. therefor _____ _____
4. neccessary _____ _____
5. recieve _____ _____

ISBN: 978-1-897457-05-4

6.   heros   _____   _____

7.   success   _____   _____

8.   definite   _____   _____

9.   professer   _____   _____

10. occurence   _____   _____

F.   Underline the correct homonym in each of the sentences below.

1.   They looked for (their / there / they're) bus tickets.

2.   His (presence / presents) was expected at the meeting.

3.   (Who's / Whose) shoes were left in the hall?

4.   The (plane / plain) was full so they took the train.

5.   The (herd / heard) of cattle stampeded.

6.   The school (principal / principle) addressed the student body.

7.   She was (bored / board) with the book she was reading.

8.   The players complained that the rule change was not (fare / fair).

G.   Underline the correct word in each of the following sentences.

1.   He likes (these / this) type of car.

2.   (That / Those) types of exercises are strenuous.

3.   She did not feel (good / well) so she went home to rest.

4.   They had a (well / good) time at the fun fair.

5.   He felt (badly / bad) that he couldn't stay longer.

6.   She played (badly / bad) and lost the match.

7.   She ate (less / fewer) food than anyone else.

8.   The teacher gave (less / fewer) homework this weekend.

9.   He drank (less / fewer) cans of pop than his friend.

10. They had (less / fewer) of a wait for the morning bus.

H. In the space provided, enter the root word for each word below.

1. decision   _____

2. occurrence   _____

3. outrageous   _____

4. production   _____

5. negligence   _____

6. identification   _____

I. Match the word in bold in each phrase with its synonym.

1. **tolerable** pain _____		A. incapable
2. **momentous** occasion _____		B. stubborn
3. **incompetent** driver _____		C. bearable
4. **repulsive** monster _____		D. well-known
5. **prominent** world leader _____		E. important
6. **obstinate** person _____		F. dangerous
7. **laborious** task _____		G. incredible
8. **hazardous** driving _____		H. pitiful
9. **extraordinary** sight _____		I. disgusting
10. **pathetic** mishap _____		J. difficult

J. Underline the synonym for each word below from the list.

1. **hazardous**	awful	bumpy	smooth	dangerous
2. **roomy**	spacious	hollow	wide	empty
3. **ugly**	scary	hideous	strange	odd
4. **difficult**	entertaining	challenging	necessary	important
5. **loud**	entertaining	deafening	smooth	rough
6. **glided**	splashed	dipped	crashed	floated

ISBN: 978-1-897457-05-4

K. Give a homonym for each word below. Be careful to spell the homonym correctly.

1. pores – _____

2. break – _____

3. read – _____

4. night – _____

5. aloud – _____

6. rain – _____

7. weigh – _____

8. sail – _____

L. For each topic sentence below, add two or three more sentences to make a complete paragraph.

1. We had a hearty Thanksgiving dinner.

_____

_____

_____

_____

2. We were down to the last batter at the bottom of the ninth inning, trailing by one run.

_____

_____

_____

_____

3. The courier handed me a heavy parcel.

_____

_____

_____

_____

The COLUMBIA ICEFIELD

COLUMBIA ICEFIELD is <u>situated</u> on the <u>boundary</u> of Jasper and Banff national parks and covers an area of over 325 square kilometres. The Icefield is made of solid ice 350 metres thick. Its melt waters feed three oceans: the Arctic, the Atlantic, and the Pacific. At the <u>base</u> of the Columbia Icefield is the Athabasca Glacier which is <u>approximately</u> 6 kilometres in length and 1 kilometre wide.

Because this glacier is easily <u>accessible</u>, tourists <u>venture</u> out onto the glacier in a specially designed vehicle called a Snocoach. The Snocoach is equipped with low pressure tires for <u>traction</u> and can transport 55 tourists to and from the centre of the Icefield. Once in the middle, the tourists can step out onto this Icefield formed from falling snow that has <u>accumulated</u> for over 400 years. To the visitor, the Columbia Icefield appears to sit perfectly still. Actually, it is in constant motion to and fro shaping the landscape. This back and forth movement takes thousands of years and is so <u>gradual</u> that it is only <u>detectable</u> through scientific research.

Although the Icefield is made up of a thick layer of ice, it is home to both plants and animals. Grizzly bears have winter dens near the Icefield and are frequently seen in the spring and fall seasons. Plants take many years to <u>establish</u> themselves in this <u>harsh</u> <u>environment</u>. To protect both the plants and animals of the area, strict rules of <u>conservation</u> are <u>enforced</u>. Tourists are asked not to feed the animals as it can actually shorten their lives. Visitors are asked to use specially <u>designed</u> footpaths to avoid trampling the plant life.

The Columbia Icefield is truly a wonder and is enjoyed by thousands of visitors each year. Hikers, campers, cyclists, and motorists take advantage of the natural beauty of the wildlife, rivers, mountains, and lakes of this <u>breath-taking</u> region.

   ISBN: 978-1-897457-05-4

Re-read the passage paying particular attention to the underlined words and their meanings in context.

A. **Enter the words from the passage that best suit the meanings below.**

1. _____ takes place slowly, over time

2. _____ grip, friction

3. _____ rough, tough, difficult

4. _____ awesome, spectacular, wonderful

5. _____ place of nature, defined area

6. _____ easy to get to, available

7. _____ roughly, close to, near in estimate

8. _____ located, placed

9. _____ border, edge of, limit of

10. _____ built up, added up, piled up

11. _____ build, form, grow, locate, situate, put in place

12. _____ bottom, ground level

13. _____ go out into, investigate, discover

14. _____ able to be found

15. _____ applied

16. _____ drawn, formulated, built, created

17. _____ preservation, guarding wildlife

 **Working with Facts**

B. State two facts from each paragraph in the passage entitled "The Columbia Icefield".

Paragraph One

1. _____

2. _____

Paragraph Two

1. _____

2. _____

Paragraph Three

1. _____

2. _____

Paragraph Four

1. _____

2. _____

Creating a Factual Composition

C. Read the list of facts about grizzly bears. Write a two-paragraph composition using these facts. Add your own ideas to make it interesting.

* Grizzly bears can outrun human beings.
* Grizzly bears are the largest mountain animals.
* Mountain lions are afraid of grizzly bears.
* A grizzly bear might weigh up to 230 kilograms (500 pounds).
* Grizzly bears can run up to 50 kilometres an hour.
* Grizzly bears hibernate in the winter and wake up in the spring.

ISBN: 978-1-897457-05-4

- Grizzly bears are omnivorous (they eat both plants and animals).
- Grizzly bears eat fish.
- Grizzly bears grow to be 9 feet standing upright.
- Grizzly bears have exceptional sense of smell, good hearing, and are powerful.
- Grizzly bears are shy around human beings but will attack if their food or young are threatened.
- Never run away from a bear; give way by backing up slowly.
- Never surprise a bear; always make noises to let it know you're nearby.
- Store food safely at your campsite.

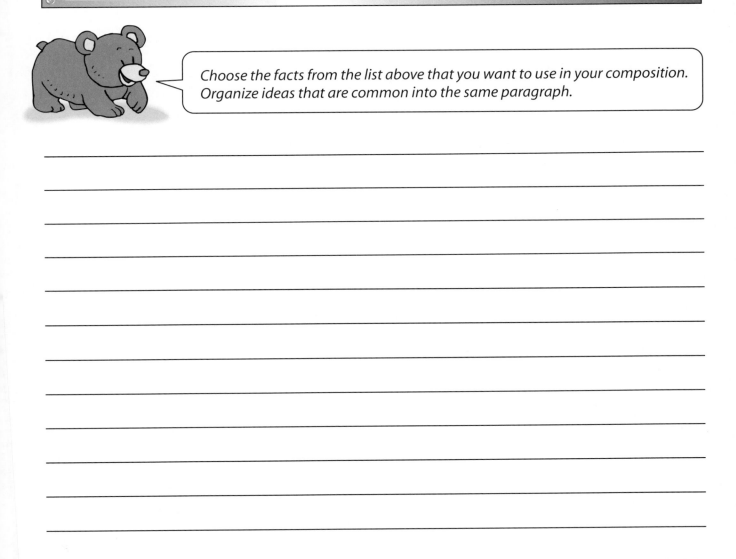

Choose the facts from the list above that you want to use in your composition. Organize ideas that are common into the same paragraph.

9 Haiku Poetry

Haiku is a Japanese form of poetry that is highly descriptive. It often deals with single ideas, descriptions, or moments. The standard format is three lines with a total number of syllables for each line as follows: 5 – 7 – 5 for a total of 17 syllables.

Example: running jumping child
flying swooping soaring high
imagining flight

This simple haiku poem is about a child who is moving about but in his mind, he is in flight. It is about imagination. Notice the words ending in "ing" (verbals) used together to create a consistent effect. Note also the simplicity of topic – one single idea.

A. **Before writing your haiku poems, follow these exercises.**

Word association

On the **first** line, make a list of five <u>action words</u> associated with each of the following ideas.

On the **second** line, write <u>descriptive words</u> of colour, sound, smell, or shape that are associated with the senses for that subject.

On the **third** line, write <u>items</u> that are associated with each topic.

Example:

Swimming

Action:	1. splashing	2. diving	3. floating	4. sinking	5. plunging
Sensory:	1. blue	2. fresh	3. cool	4. deep	5. chilly
Items:	1. towel	2. sand	3. wind	4. waves	5. surf board

ISBN: 978-1-897457-05-4

Dining out

Action: 1. _____ 2. _____ 3. _____ 4. _____ 5. _____

Sensory: 1. _____ 2. _____ 3. _____ 4. _____ 5. _____

Items: 1. _____ 2. _____ 3. _____ 4. _____ 5. _____

Schoolyard

Action: 1. _____ 2. _____ 3. _____ 4. _____ 5. _____

Sensory: 1. _____ 2. _____ 3. _____ 4. _____ 5. _____

Items: 1. _____ 2. _____ 3. _____ 4. _____ 5. _____

Birthday party

Action: 1. _____ 2. _____ 3. _____ 4. _____ 5. _____

Sensory: 1. _____ 2. _____ 3. _____ 4. _____ 5. _____

Items: 1. _____ 2. _____ 3. _____ 4. _____ 5. _____

Hockey

Action: 1. _____ 2. _____ 3. _____ 4. _____ 5. _____

Sensory: 1. _____ 2. _____ 3. _____ 4. _____ 5. _____

Items: 1. _____ 2. _____ 3. _____ 4. _____ 5. _____

 **Writing Haiku Poems**

B. From the lists you created in (A), choose two topics to compose Haiku poems. Create an interesting title for each.

Poem A

_____

_____

_____

_____

Poem B

_____

_____

_____

_____

C. Here is a list of words with the number of syllables in parentheses. Use some of these words in addition to your own to form Haiku poetry.

Group the words that best suit your topic. For example, if you are composing a poem about night, you may use the following words: midnight, mysterious, scary, sky, lonely, moonlight, stars, clouds, black...

shimmering	(3)	midnight	(2)	scary	(2)
beautiful	(3)	golden	(2)	glow	(1)
mysterious	(4)	whispering	(3)	sad	(1)
		laughing	(2)	bright	(1)
		happiness	(3)	sky	(1)
		happy	(2)	lonely	(2)
		flowing	(2)	castles	(2)

ISBN: 978-1-897457-05-4

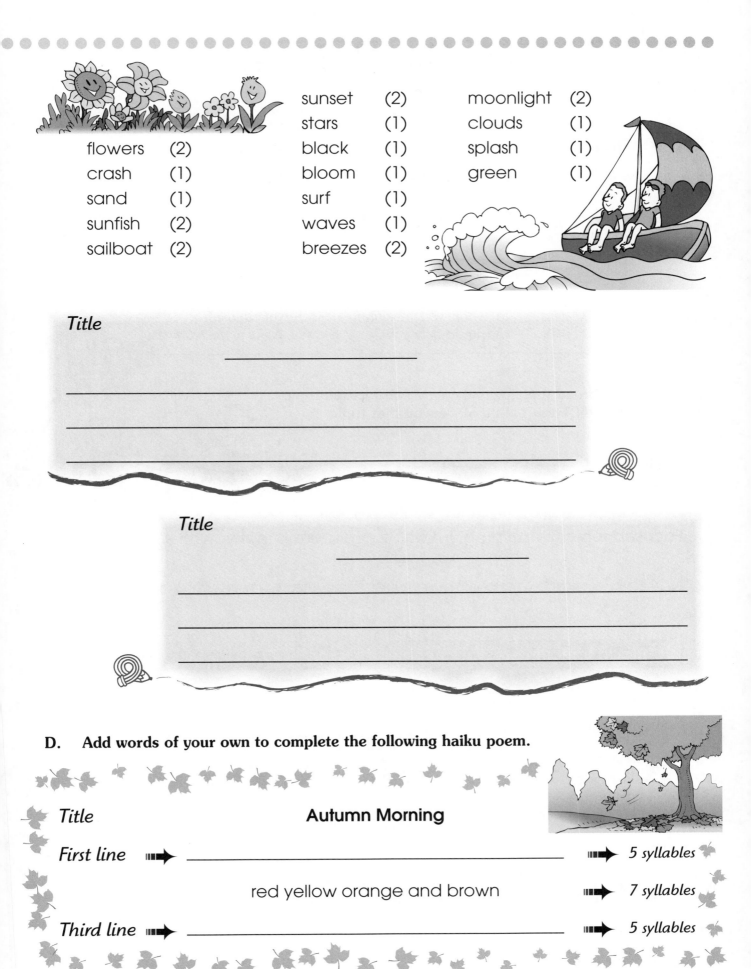

flowers (2)
crash (1)
sand (1)
sunfish (2)
sailboat (2)

sunset (2)
stars (1)
black (1)
bloom (1)
surf (1)
waves (1)
breezes (2)

moonlight (2)
clouds (1)
splash (1)
green (1)

Title

_____

_____

_____

_____

Title

_____

_____

_____

_____

D.   Add words of your own to complete the following haiku poem.

Title   **Autumn Morning**

First line ➡ _____   ➡ *5 syllables*

red yellow orange and brown   ➡ *7 syllables*

Third line ➡ _____   ➡ *5 syllables*

ISBN: 978-1-897457-05-4

10 Narrative Writing

Narrative writing is to tell a brief story. It is structured in three parts:

(a) Beginning – topic sentence; this is the controlling idea of your story
(b) Middle – the details that support your topic
(c) End – the conclusion to reinforce the controlling idea

The three "Ws" of writing:
1. *What* – *the controlling idea of your story*
2. *Who* – *for whom you are writing the story; your audience*
3. *Why* – *the purpose for your story; why it is useful to the reader*

A. **For each broad topic below, create two focused topics that offer different points of view on that topic.**

Example: Broad topic: Team sports

Focused topic A: Playing a team sport teaches the importance of working with others.

Focused topic B: The problem with team sports is that you must depend on others to succeed.

Notice how each focused topic takes the writer in a different direction.

---

1 **Broad topic: Interesting Summer Holidays**

Focused topic A: _____

Focused topic B: _____

2 **Broad topic: Having a Pet**

Focused topic A: _____

Focused topic B: _____

3 **Broad topic: Preparing for the First Day of School**

Focused topic A: _____

Focused topic B: _____

 ISBN: 978-1-897457-05-4

(4) Broad topic: Birthday Celebration

Focused topic A: _____

_____

_____

Focused topic B: _____

_____

(5) Broad topic: My Favourite Room in my House

Focused topic A: _____

Focused topic B: _____

(6) Broad topic: Relatives Come for a Visit

Focused topic A: _____

Focused topic B: _____

(7) Broad topic: Scary Movies

Focused topic A: _____

Focused topic B: _____

(8) Broad topic: Making New Friends

Focused topic A: _____

Focused topic B: _____

(9) Broad topic: Summer Camp

Focused topic A: _____

Focused topic B: _____

(10) Broad topic: Competitive Sports

Focused topic A: _____

Focused topic B: _____

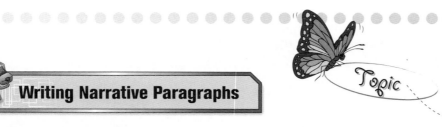

Writing Narrative Paragraphs

Topic   *Topic sentence*

B. Use two of the topics above to tell of an incident, a memory, or an event.

PARAGRAPH ONE

Topic: _____

Topic sentence: ⟵ *Introduces your focused topic*

_____

Developmental sentences: ⟵ *Build your story from details*

_____

_____

_____

_____

_____

_____

_____

_____

_____

_____

Conclusion: ⟵ *Story ending: reason for writing; restates your controlling idea*

_____

_____

_____

ISBN: 978-1-897457-05-4

Developmental sentences   *Conclusion*

PARAGRAPH TWO

Topic: _____

Topic sentence: ⟵ *Introduces your focused topic*

_____

Developmental sentences: ⟵ *Build your story from details*

_____

_____

_____

_____

_____

_____

_____

_____

_____

Conclusion: ⟵ *Story ending: reason for writing; restates your controlling idea*

_____

_____

_____

11 Vocabulary Development

 **Root Word Quiz**

A. Use the clue to discover the new word developed from the word given.

Example:

hair – a design or style – hairdo

1. stamp – cattle gone wild – _____

2. relate – a cousin or an aunt, for example – _____

3. try – happens in a courtroom – _____

4. camp – the location of your tent – _____

5. cycle – one who rides a bike – _____

6. attract – to take away one's attention – _____

7. collide – when two vehicles crash – _____

8. sense – silliness – _____

9. capture – one who gets caught – _____

10. victor – how to describe the winner – _____

11. fix – encloses the light bulb – _____

12. pair – to fix something – _____

13. incidence – happen at the same time – _____

14. collect – art or stamps, for example – _____

15. snow – travels over the snow – _____

16. coincide – happen at the same time – _____

 ISBN: 978-1-897457-05-4

17. nature – comes from nature – _____

18. comic – when it's funny, it's – _____

19. auto – works on its own – _____

20. arrange – to arrange again or differently – _____

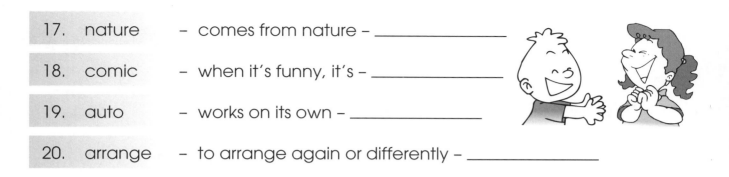

Transitional Words and Conjunctions

Transitional words join short sentences by making one subordinate to the other – that is, one depends on the other for full meaning.

Example: John walked home. His father couldn't pick him up from school.
              Because his father couldn't pick him up from school, John walked home.

Conjunctions such as "and", "or", and "but" also join sentences.

Example: John wanted to walk home. His father picked him up from school.
              John wanted to walk home **but** his father picked him up from school.

B.   **Join each of the following short sentences with either a transitional word or a conjunction from the word bank below.**

| because | but | when | if | once | although | so |
| as soon as | after | then | while | even though |

1.   Mary called her friend on the telephone. She got no answer.

   _____

2.   The game was over. Everyone went home.

   _____

3.   You come over to my house.   We can play computer games.

   _____

11

4. The storm was over. The sun came out.

    _____

5. He waited for hours for his friends to show up. It started to get dark.

    _____

6. The school bell rang. Summer holidays had started.

    _____

7. He was the team captain. He had to be a leader.

    _____

8. They ate dinner. They had dessert.

    _____

    _____

9. His new bike was very fast. It was too big for him.

    _____

10. His alarm went off. He was late for school.

    _____

11. They were the first to arrive. They still waited a long time in line.

    _____

    _____

12. They were camping in the mountains. A bear visited their campsite.

    _____

    _____

ISBN: 978-1-897457-05-4

C. In each of the following sentences, provide a subordinate clause that suits the meaning of the sentence in the space after the transitional word.

Example:

Although _____it started to rain_____ , they went swimming anyway.

1. After they _____ , they stopped for lunch.

2. Even though the students _____ , they still had trouble finishing the assignment.

3. While they _____ , their friends cheered them on.

4. If she _____ , she will win the trophy.

5. Because he _____ , he stayed home from school.

6. Since he _____ , he has had trouble walking.

D. Add the main clause to each of the sentences below.

1. After they finished eating the whole pie, they _____ _____ .

2. Whenever the sisters go shopping, they always _____ .

3. Because they were best friends, they always _____ .

4. He would have won the game but he _____ .

5. Even though she studied for the test, she _____ .

6. She bought a new dress and she _____ .

7. Either you stay at home tonight or _____ .

8. If there is a large snowfall, we will _____ .

ISBN: 978-1-897457-05-4

12 Expository Writing

An **expository paragraph** is often written to explain something, to give the reader information, or to persuade the reader about a certain idea.

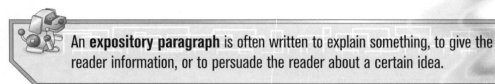

Building a **Campfire**

Although sitting around a campfire is one of the great joys of camping, building a long lasting, roaring campfire is not a simple task. Often campers simply pile up a few twigs, drop on a couple of logs, stuff in a few rolls of newspaper, and ignite. Unfortunately, they may be disappointed when the fire blazes momentarily, then extinguishes itself just as quickly. The first step in building a campfire is to gather numerous dry twigs and bark shavings and create a pile. Next, add small sticks around your pile in a tepee-like fashion. The tepee shape allows air to get in underneath the pile which the fire needs to maintain a flame. Build the pile by adding larger twigs and sticks; be sure to keep the tepee shape. Find an opening and ignite the dry bark shavings and twigs used as the base of your pile. As the fire builds, add larger pieces of wood.

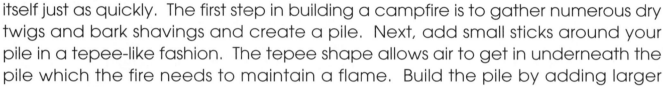

Keep to the writing format of: Topic Sentence + Body Sentences + Conclusion.

Never simply toss logs on to the pile as it will flatten your tepee shape and no air will get in below the pile. At this point you should be enjoying a roaring fire but be mindful to add wood consistently to maintain enough fuel to keep your fire going.

A. Identify the following in "Building a Campfire".

1. Purpose of writing "Building a Campfire": _____

   _____

2. Topic sentence: _____

   _____

3. Concluding sentence: _____

   _____

                    ISBN: 978-1-897457-05-4

Summer in the City

When the summer arrives, many people look forward to leaving the city. However, the city offers a variety of interesting ways to spend the hot, lazy days of summer. For those of you who find sitting around a cottage in the middle of the wilderness boring, consider what the city has to offer. When the weather gets unbearably hot, visit one of the many outdoor swimming pools. Or, spend the afternoon in a cool, dark, air-conditioned movie theatre. If you're a cyclist, you can travel the parkland trails that crisscross the city. A visit to the zoo is always interesting, particularly since many newborn animals have arrived in the spring. For the sporting type, there is free tennis at city courts, volleyball at the beach, and skateboarding at a number of specially designed facilities. In fact, you could choose a different activity almost every day. If you should run out of things to do, visit the local mall. There, you can browse record stores, get an ice cream treat, check out the latest computer games, or window shop the latest fashions. Whatever your preference, the city in the summer is a lively place with something for everyone.

B.   Identify the following in "Summer in the City".

1.   Purpose of writing "Summer in the City": _____

_____

2.   Topic sentence: _____

_____

3.   Concluding sentence: _____

_____

Challenge

Provide a concluding sentence of your own for "Summer in the City".

_____

12

C. **Compose an explanatory paragraph using one of the following topics.**

Assume that the person to whom you are writing needs the information you are offering.

The best place to do homework
The best way to learn how to swim
Using the Internet
Making the perfect sandwich
Taking care of a pet

Topic: _____

Topic sentence:

_____

Body sentences:

_____

_____

_____

_____

_____

_____

_____

_____

Concluding sentence:

_____

_____

_____

ISBN: 978-1-897457-05-4

D. **Compose a persuasive paragraph using one of the following topics.**

Rollerblading is the best exercise.

Swimming in a pool is better than swimming on a lake.

Schools give too much homework.

Summer holidays are too long.

It's great having an older brother (or sister).

Topic: _____

Topic sentence:

_____

Body sentences:

_____

_____

_____

_____

_____

_____

_____

_____

Concluding sentence:

_____

_____

_____

In the <u>realm</u> of gnomes and fairies, two small gnomes were always <u>cooking up</u> ways to make easy money, but all they seemed to cause was <u>mischief</u>.

It was April Fools' Day and the gnomes had an idea. When a fairy named Frieda flew by with her heavy head and tired wings, the gnomes <u>sprung into action</u>. "Power for sale! Power for sale!" they called out. Frieda's ears <u>perked up</u>. "This is just what I need," she thought. Lately, she had not been sleeping well and was feeling quite <u>feeble</u>. The gnomes <u>convinced</u> her that by keeping their special pebble in her pocket, she would have power and energy. So, Frieda bought the little grey pebble, and the <u>gleeful</u> gnomes pocketed Frieda's five dollars.

Soon, word spread to other fairies, and the gnomes sold two more pebbles: one that promised luck and one that <u>guaranteed</u> courage. Fifteen dollars <u>better off</u> now, the gnomes saw an <u>opportunity</u>: they could open a store and sell pebbles that promised things like talent, beauty, and hope. They would be rich!

But then something happened to bring the gnomes back to <u>reality</u>. Frieda lost her pebble! Before she knew it was lost, though, she walked around with much power as she had when it was safe in her pocket. She <u>realized</u> that she did not <u>derive</u> the power from the tiny pebble after all. It must have come from the sleep she was finally getting! Feeling foolish, Frieda went to her fairy friends.

ISBN: 978-1-897457-05-4

Together, they <u>tramped</u> up to the gnomes. "The pebble you sold me doesn't give luck!" said one fairy. "This pebble doesn't give courage at all!" another fairy <u>complained</u>.

Then Frieda, thinking that she had the power to change the ways of the <u>deceitful</u> gnomes, said, "For you I have only pity. You have talent and imagination, yet you waste them on silly <u>swindles</u>. You might be making fast money, but you will lose your friends. Everyone will know that you are not honest."

The gnomes listened. After much thought, they put down their pebbles and picked up paintbrushes – to make <u>magnificent</u> paintings, and sell their beautiful works to their many, many friends.

 **Words in Context**

Read the story and match the underlined words with the meanings from the list according to the "context" of the sentences in which they appear.

Paragraph One

1. realm ____   2. cooking up ____   3. mischief ____

A. inventing
B. kingdom
C. playful behaviour that causes minor trouble

Use each of the following words in a sentence to show its meaning.

realm

_____

mischief

_____

Paragraph Two

1. sprung into action ____
2. perked up ____
3. feeble ____
4. convinced ____
5. gleeful ____

A. very happy
B. began doing something quickly and with energy
C. weak
D. made one believe
E. raised or stuck up quickly

Use each of the following words in a sentence to show its meaning.

feeble

_____

gleeful

_____

Paragraph Three

1. guaranteed ____
2. better off ____
3. opportunity ____

A. richer
B. good chance for success
C. assured; promised

Use each of the following words in a sentence to show its meaning.

guaranteed

_____

opportunity

_____

Paragraph Four

1. reality _____
2. realized _____
3. derive _____
4. tramped _____
5. complained _____

A. marched; walked heavily
B. understood clearly and completely
C. the quality or state of being real
D. get
E. stated that one is unhappy or dissatisfied with something

Use each of the following words in a sentence to show its meaning.

realized

_____

complained

_____

Paragraphs Five and Six

1. deceitful _____
2. swindles _____
3. magnificent _____

A. dishonest
B. very beautiful
C. acts of cheating one out of money

Use each of the following words in a sentence to show its meaning.

deceitful

_____

magnificent

_____

14 Informal Writing

Informal writing does not always follow precise rules of grammar. The sentence structure of informal writing is often quite casual. People write informally in emails, notes, friendly letters, invitations, thank you notes, or on greeting cards.

A.   Rewrite the following postcard note to make it informal.

Dear Dana,

Today we arrived in Dublin and my cousins came to meet us at the airport. I'm really excited about meeting all our relatives. Tomorrow we will travel to Cork City, and later on, we will tour the Ring of Kerry. Ireland is beautiful; the scenery is breath taking.

We have only been here a few hours but I think I'm already developing an Irish accent. My cousins think that I speak with a Canadian accent – whatever that is. For the third week of this holiday, we will be visiting more relatives in London. I hope all is well with you. I will write again soon.

Sincerely,
Lauren

Dana Shank

123 Popular Street

Toronto, Ontario

C2W V3X

Dana Shank

123 Popular Street

Toronto, Ontario

C2W V3X

ISBN: 978-1-897457-05-4

The Utterance

An utterance is an incomplete sentence that offers a complete thought. Utterances are acceptable in dialogue and informal writing.

Example: Do you want a ride home? No, thanks.
"No, thanks" is an utterance because it does not have a subject or a verb but it offers a complete thought.

Informal writing with brief sentences or utterances is particularly useful when you have limited space such as in notes or postcards.

B. **Assume you are on holiday in a place you've dreamt of visiting. Write a postcard to a friend or family member giving as many details as possible in a small space.**

14

C. Compose an invitation to a birthday party. Include all the necessary details such as date, time, place, and any other details. Use a large, bold title to announce the event.

ISBN: 978-1-897457-05-4

Want Ads

Newspapers often charge by the words for advertisements. To save space, complete sentences are not used. Note that the ad below gives details about the product and it also adds the statement "great deal" to try to entice the buyer.

10-speed Road Racer for Sale

Boy's 10-speed road racer. Red with white detailing. New tires, include lock. Excellent shape. Great deal. Asking $75.00.

D. Assume that you are trying to sell something. Write ads for two of the following products:

a.	your desktop computer	b.	your disc player
c.	your skis	d.	a puppy from the new litter
e.	a computer game	f.	your old skateboard
g.	a doll collection	h.	music CDs

1.

2.

15 Synonyms – Facts about Canada

In each of the following paragraphs, the words in bold can be replaced by synonyms numbered below. Place the number of the replacement synonym beside the word in bold.

The History of Canadian Flags

The first Canadian flag was likely the St. George's Cross, a fifteenth century English flag. John Cabot reached the east coast of Canada in 1497 and erected the flag claiming the land for England. In 1534, Jacques Cartier **hoisted** ◯ the fleur-de-lis firmly **establishing** ◯ French **sovereignty** ◯ in Canada. In the early 1760's, Canada was **ceded** ◯ to the United Kingdom and the Royal Union flag, more commonly known as the Union Jack, became the **official** ◯ flag of Canada.

1 setting up   **2** raised   **3** rule

4 surrendered   **5** standard

The Red Ensign flag, a cross between the Union Jack and a shield bearing the arms of Nova Scotia, Ontario, New Brunswick, and Quebec, **originated** ◯ as a Merchant Marine flag in 1707. Never **officially** ◯ **acknowledged** ◯ as the flag of Canada on land, the British admiralty accepted the Red Ensign as the official Canadian **maritime** ◯ flag. In 1924, the Order of Council changed the unofficial Red Ensign replacing the **original** ◯ shield with the Canadian Coat of Arms. A government order in 1945 **declared** ◯ this new

ISBN: 978-1-897457-05-4

version ◯ to be the interim flag of Canada until a new one was **designed** ◯ .
In 1965, the Canadian Ensign was replaced by the current red and white maple
leaf flag that is the proud **symbol** ◯ of Canada.

6	nautical or marine	**7**	began	**8**	accepted
9	announced	**10**	formally	**11**	type
12	representation	**13**	first	**14**	created

Nunavut
Canada's New Territory

Nunavut, Canada's newest **territory** ◯ , gets its name
from the Inuktitut word meaning "our land". Nunavut officially became a territory
on April 1, 1999. This vast region **extends** ◯ northwest from Hudson Bay beyond
the tree line to the North Pole. In all, Nunavut's **expanse** ◯ is an **astounding** ◯
2,000,000 square kilometres.

The Nunavut landscape is **remarkably** ◯ **diverse** ◯ . The North Baffin
region is a mixture of mountain ranges and fiords while the Kivalliq area is flat.

15	stretches	**16**	surprisingly	**17**	shocking
18	region	**19**	vastness	**20**	assorted

Nunavut's population is the youngest in Canada – its median age is only 22
years. The population is growing rapidly with an **impressive** ◯ 10% increase
since its **inception** ◯ in 1999. Most of the Nunavut population is made up of the

Inuit people. There are 26 communities in Nunavut including its capital, Iqaluit, which has a population of close to 6,000. Many Nunavut communities are not **accessible** ◯ by road or rail. Basic needs including food and fuel must be **transported** ◯ by plane. Consequently, goods are very expensive. Most citizens of Nunavut are **employed** ◯ by the three levels of government: municipal, federal, and territorial. As new industries develop, particularly in the mining **sector** ◯ , more job **opportunities** ◯ will **emerge** ◯ . There is also growth in fisheries and tourism, and there is a growing interest in Inuit art, **particularly** ◯ stone carvings and prints.

21 hired	**22** division or section	**23** appear
24 beginning	**25** extraordinary	**26** approachable
27 sent	**28** chances	**29** especially

The people of Nunavut speak four languages (French, English, Inuinaqtun, and Inuktitut), live in an area that is one-fifth the size of Canada, and have an extremely low population **density** ◯ . It is a challenge for the federal government to meet the **unique** ◯ needs of the region. **Primary** ◯ concerns for the government of Canada in this region are health, education, and job creation. Although Nunavut presents **unprecedented** ◯ challenges, the people of Nunavut remain **optimistic** ◯ .

| **30** first | **31** thickness | **32** different or special |
| **33** new | **34** confident | |

ISBN: 978-1-897457-05-4

The Canadian National Anthem — "O Canada"

The Official Lyrics of "O Canada"

O Canada!
Our home and native land!
True patriot love in all thy sons command.

With glowing hearts we see thee rise,
The True North strong and free!

From far and wide,
O Canada, we stand on guard for thee.

God keep our land glorious and free!
O Canada, we stand on guard for thee.

O Canada, we stand on guard for thee.

Our national anthem, as we know it today, became the official anthem on July 1, 1980. However, the **initial** ◯ singing of this song took place 100 years **prior** ◯. Calixa Lavallée, a renowned **composer** ◯ of his time, is credited with composing the music to **accompany** ◯ the French lyrics written by Sir Adolphe-Basil Routhier. Over the years there have been **numerous** ◯ English **renditions** ◯ of the song but the lyrics of Robert Stanley Weir, written in 1908, became the official English version. This version remained **unaltered** ◯ until 1968 when the Canadian government made **minor** ◯ changes. The French version has remained unchanged.

35 unchanged		**36** small		**37** first	
	38 many		**39** before		
40 versions		**41** song-writer		**42** go along with	

PROGRESS TEST 2

A. Use the context of each of the sentences below to determine the meaning of the italicized word. Circle the best synonym from the list provided.

1. The table was *situated* in the centre of the room.

   located   placed   found   left

2. The *boundary* of the playing field was fenced.

   place   limitations   area   situation

3. They set up camp at the *base* of the mountain.

   apex   centre   edge   bottom

4. The time was *approximately* four o'clock.

   nearly   always   forever   exactly

5. The room was *accessible* by a door off the hall.

   barred   available   cut off   approachable

6. His dog will *venture* into the street if not leashed.

   slip   wander   fall   cross

7. For *traction* he wore spiked shoes.

   speed   grip   style   efficiency

8. He *accumulated* all his money from working many jobs.

   gathered   collected   earned   found

9. The melting of the ice was *gradual* in the morning sun.

   sudden   abrupt   slow   wet

10. The cell was only *detectable* through a microscope.

    known   accessible   visible   shown

11. They will *establish* an award table near the track and field events.

    organize   set up   build   create

12. The rain and wind of the unusually *harsh* weather stopped the play-day.

    difficult   rough   balmy   rugged

ISBN: 978-1-897457-05-4

13. He was concerned for the *environment* particularly the preservation of forests.

surroundings   location   place   neighbourhood

14. The *conservation* of wildlife in their natural habitat is important.

survival   protection   neglect   concern

15. The rules of the game were *enforced* by the referee.

applied   altered   declined   forgotten

16. The architect *designed* a model of the office tower.

destroyed   created   built   changed

B. Give one focused topic sentence for each of the following general topics.

1. Computer Games

_____

_____

2. Exercise

_____

_____

3. Junk Food

_____

_____

4. Shopping for a Birthday Present

_____

_____

5. Music

_____

_____

C. State the root word for each word below.

1. statement _____
2. coincidence _____
3. relationship _____
4. attraction _____
5. captive _____
6. collision _____
7. sensibility _____
8. incidentally _____
9. victorious _____
10. repairing _____

D. Join the following pairs of sentences with either a conjunction or a transitional adverb from the list below.

Use each conjunction only once.

as soon as   although   while   and   because

1. He walked home. He missed the school bus.

   _____

2. She invited her friends over for a sleepover. They ordered pizza.

   _____

3. The game continued. It was raining.

   _____

4. He cooked hot dogs. She set the table.

   _____

5. The teacher began teaching. The students were seated at their desks.

   _____

   _____

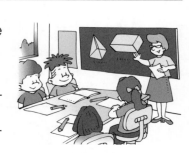

E. **Match the italicized words with their meanings. A brief phrase is given to add context to each of the italicized words.**

Group A

1. *concoct* an idea

2. *dominate* the race

3. *fascination* of the fans

4. 100th *anniversary*

5. *consecutive* victories

6. *culminating* at the finish line

7. *signifying* the winner

8. an amazing *feat* of strength

9. *reserved* for the winner

10. from city to *rural* area

A   ending

B   countryside

C   yearly celebration

D   accomplishment

E   awe, surprise

F   saved

G   many in a row

H   indicating

I   come up with, develop

J   control, take over

Group B

1. *individual* time trial

2. *accumulated* time

3. *overcome* difficulty

4. *admired* by everyone

5. *endurance* to continue the race

6. *determination* to succeed

7. mountain *terrain*

8. training *vigorously*

9. *pursuit* of victory

10. *glorious* retirement

A   get over, solve

B   strength, ability

C   landscape, country

D   bringing great fame

E   total of, added up

F   strenuously, with great effort

G   for one person

H   quest for, search for

I   loved

J   desire

ISBN: 978-1-897457-05-4

F.   Match each of the words on the left with its synonym.

1.   hoisted

2.   establishing

3.   impressive

4.   diverse

5.   optimistic

6.   declared

7.   version

8.   maritime

9.   inception

10.   accessible

A beginning
B extraordinary
C raised
D assorted
E setting up
F type
G nautical
H announced
I confident
J approachable

G.   Re-write each of the following sentences, using a more descriptive synonym or phrase to replace the underlined word.

1.   The <u>house</u> is the biggest in the neighbourhood.

_____

2.   Uncle Jeff's <u>car</u> ran on both gasoline and electricity.

_____

3.   We were <u>happy</u> that our team finally won.

_____

4.   We could hardly stand the <u>loud</u> music.

_____

5.   Everyone enjoyed the <u>good</u> show.

_____

H. Compose an expository paragraph on the following topic.

Topic: The Best Time of the Year

Topic Sentence:

_____

_____

Body Sentences:

_____

_____

_____

_____

_____

_____

_____

_____

Concluding Sentence:

_____

_____

_____

ISBN: 978-1-897457-05-4

ISBN: 978-1-897457-05-4

ISBN: 978-1-897457-05-4

Language Games

1 Look at the pictures. Complete the Sports Crossword Puzzle.

SPORTS

Crossword Puzzle

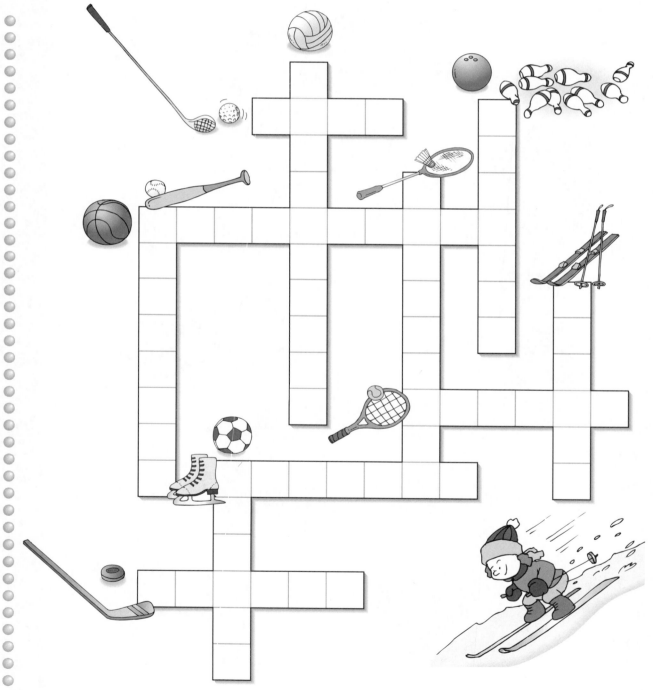

ISBN: 978-1-897457-05-4

2 Complete the word slides to turn "main" into "trap". Change only one letter for each slide.

| m | a | i | n |

↓

| ☐ | a | i | n |

↓

| ☐ | ☐ | ☐ | ☐ |

↓

| g | ☐ | i | n |

↓

| ☐ | ☐ | ☐ | ☐ |

↓

| ☐ | r | i | p |

↓

| ☐ | ☐ | ☐ | ☐ |

ISBN: 978-1-897457-05-4

3 Complete the crossword puzzle with synonyms of the clue words.

Across	**Down**
A. opportunity	1. afraid
B. clue	2. watchful
C. precise	3. use
D. fix	4. enormous
E. hop	5. fly
F. genuine	6. stop
	7. hide

Synonym Crossword Puzzle

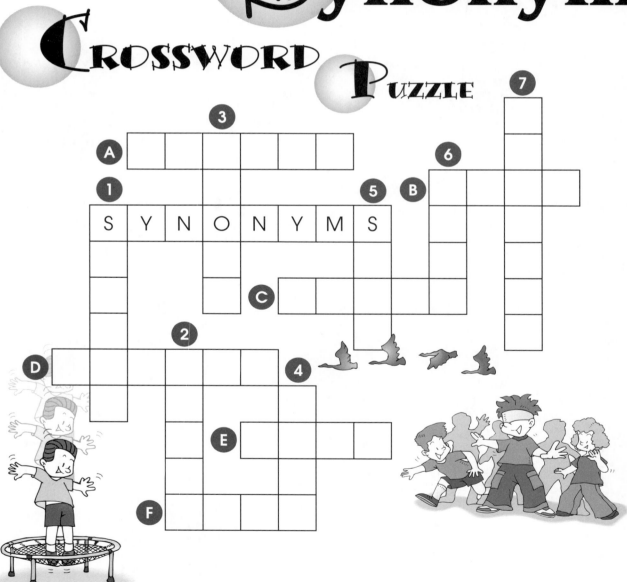

S Y N O N Y M S

ISBN: 978-1-897457-05-4

4 Fill in the missing letters to complete the words.

1.
	I	S	
A			I
R	1		L
T	I	L	

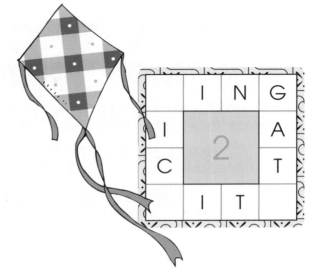

2.
	I	N	G
I			A
C	2		T
	I	T	

3.
P	E	E	
O			I
R	3		V
	A	K	

4.
	A	I	
O			E
P	4		A
V	E	R	

5.
T	H	A	
A			I
I	5		C
	O	O	

6.
	I	L	
A			A
K	6		R
A	R	N	

5 Find out what the monsters say by unscrambling the letters.

EW VILE NO A ELAPTN

ARF YAAW OFMR TAHER.

EW ATWN OT KEAM

WNE NIRFSED. NAC EW

EB ESRFIDN?

_____

_____

_____

_____

ISBN: 978-1-897457-05-4

6

Complete the crossword puzzle with antonyms of the clue words.

Antonym Crossword Puzzle

Across

A. coarse
B. relaxed
C. shrink
D. bright
E. inching
F. accept

Down

1. favourable
2. rare
3. celebrate
4. bland
5. daring
6. miserable

1. ANTONYMS

7 Complete the word slides to turn "reap" into "well". Change only one letter for each slide.

r e a p

⬜ e a p

⬜ ⬜ ⬜ ⬜

h e a ⬜

⬜ ⬜ ⬜ ⬜

s e ⬜ l

⬜ ⬜ ⬜ ⬜

   ISBN: 978-1-897457-05-4

8

Circle twelve insects in the Insect Word Search.

h	c	d	l	f	j	a	n	e	m	g	a	e
f	r	m	g	w	w	h	q	b	a	n	h	b
c	i	c	a	d	a	c	n	s	n	e	j	l
d	c	h	m	o	s	q	u	i	t	o	c	a
m	k	b	o	b	p	e	p	d	i	g	o	d
k	e	p	f	l	b	i	l	g	s	l	c	y
r	t	l	d	j	e	n	f	a	j	c	k	b
c	a	o	v	c	e	u	r	o	t	p	r	u
h	f	c	l	p	t	z	x	i	v	b	o	g
d	b	u	m	b	l	e	b	e	e	i	a	c
a	k	s	e	f	e	i	y	a	m	q	c	i
j	m	t	d	o	q	l	r	m	o	t	h	m
k	a	n	a	n	t	x	b	c	s	r	o	g

Insect Word Search

Complete the crossword puzzle with homophones of the clue words.

Homophone Crossword Puzzle

Across — row labeled: H O M O P H O N E S

Across

A. wait

B. waist

C. rose

D. pair

E. not

Down

1. which

2. face

3. eight

4. bear

5. plane

6. sail

7. wail

ISBN: 978-1-897457-05-4

Match the pictures to form compound words. Write the words on the lines.

1. 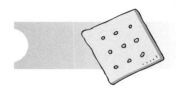   

2.    

3.    

4.    

5.    

6.    

1. _____ 2. _____

3. _____ 4. _____

5. _____ 6. _____

11 Circle twelve stationery items in the Stationery Word Search.

Stationery Word Search

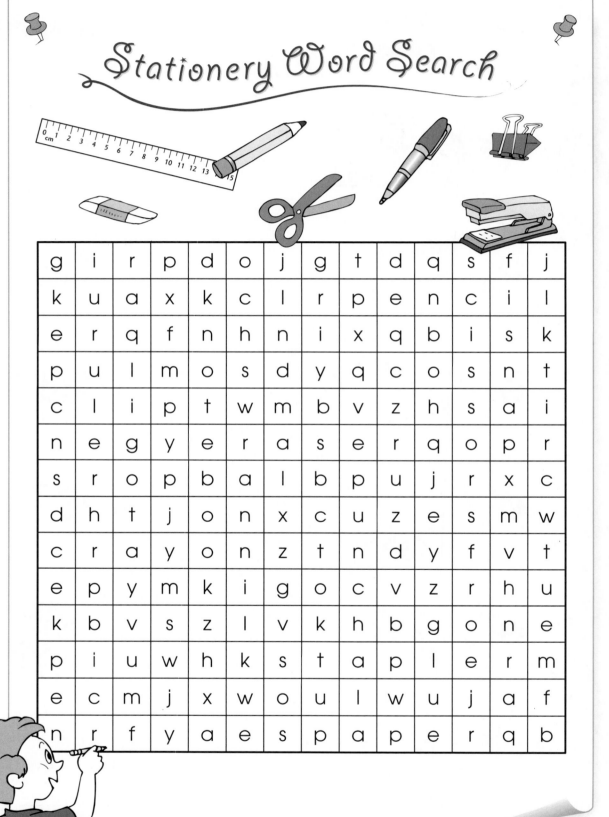

g	i	r	p	d	o	j	g	t	d	q	s	f	j
k	u	a	x	k	c	l	r	p	e	n	c	i	l
e	r	q	f	n	h	n	i	x	q	b	i	s	k
p	u	l	m	o	s	d	y	q	c	o	s	n	t
c	l	i	p	t	w	m	b	v	z	h	s	a	i
n	e	g	y	e	r	a	s	e	r	q	o	p	r
s	r	o	p	b	a	l	b	p	u	j	r	x	c
d	h	t	j	o	n	x	c	u	z	e	s	m	w
c	r	a	y	o	n	z	t	n	d	y	f	v	t
e	p	y	m	k	i	g	o	c	v	z	r	h	u
k	b	v	s	z	l	v	k	h	b	g	o	n	e
p	i	u	w	h	k	s	t	a	p	l	e	r	m
e	c	m	j	x	w	o	u	l	w	u	j	a	f
n	r	f	y	a	e	s	p	a	p	e	r	q	b

ISBN: 978-1-897457-05-4

12

Complete the crossword puzzle with synonyms of the clue words.

 **Synonym Crossword Puzzle**

Across	**Down**
A. defeat	1. strange
B. stiff	2. quick
C. damaging	3. friendly
D. grow	4. competent
E. chilly	5. slender
F. delicate	6. fortunate
G. broad	7. hard

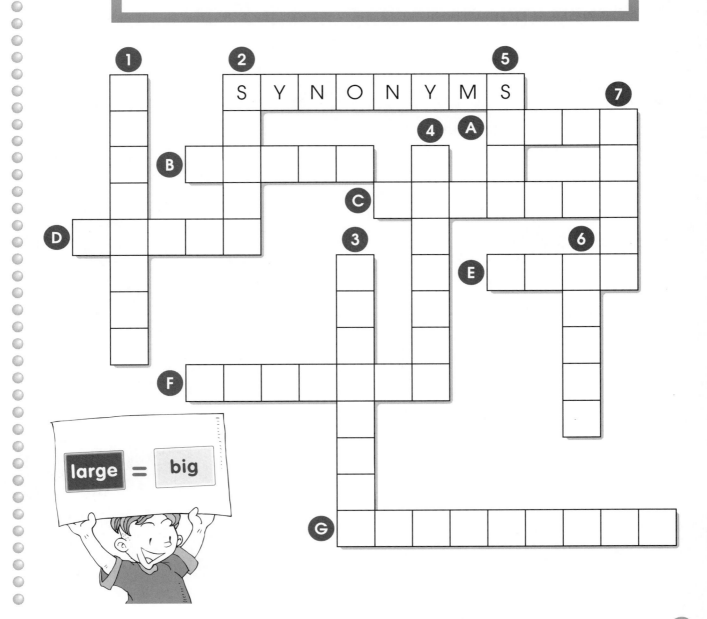

S Y N O N Y M S

large = big

ISBN: 978-1-897457-05-4

13

Complete the word slides to turn "fast" into "kite". Change only one letter for each slide.

fast

□ a s t

□ □ □ □

m □ s s

□ □ □ □

m i □ t

□ □ □ □

□ i t e

ISBN: 978-1-897457-05-4

14 Colour the correct box in each column to find out what Paula the Polar Bear says.

I	dreaming	that	me	skyed
Please	dreams	so	I	skied
May	dreamt	will	my	skiied

by	Santa Clause	in	night	?
up	Santa Claus	the	day	,
with	Santer Claus	last	thing	.

15

Complete the crossword puzzle with antonyms of the clue words.

Antonym Crossword Puzzle

Across

- A. easy
- B. shout
- C. arrive
- D. guilty
- E. decline
- F. relaxing

A N T O N Y M S

Down

1. split
2. praise
3. common
4. clear
5. sparse
6. blunt
7. pessimistic

ISBN: 978-1-897457-05-4

16

Circle ten "Halloween" words in the Holloween Word Search.

Halloween
Word Search

l	n	p	h	d	i	b	g	r	q	y	p	e	n
x	f	H	m	a	e	z	s	w	o	l	u	h	o
c	t	a	n	m	c	H	A	m	h	z	m	j	c
o	b	k	j	y	p	l	n	x	w	i	p	u	g
s	h	d	g	m	o	j	t	r	i	c	k	g	t
t	k	a	w	h	e	q	r	e	l	q	i	H	a
u	H	a	l	l	o	w	e	e	n	t	n	m	k
m	d	f	z	t	p	s	a	y	i	p	q	w	f
e	o	h	t	l	c	n	t	w	s	b	a	e	j
s	p	i	d	e	r	h	s	g	i	a	c	x	o
b	f	n	y	q	s	k	e	l	e	t	o	n	m
p	j	f	x	l	b	z	k	x	d	s	c	p	r
d	z	w	a	r	c	i	g	b	r	f	z	h	l
m	l	x	i	q	j	n	p	o	m	k	y	m	k

ISBN: 978-1-897457-05-4

1 Cats

A.
1. 60 million
2. Miacis
3. 35 million
4. 12,000
5. sabre-toothed tigers and true cats
6. cheetah
7. small cat
8. hunters
9. 41
10. cheetah

B.
1. The (tourists) from Japan visited Niagara Falls and took the Maid of the Mist boat (ride).
2. Mr. Smith taught at Maple Road Public School for twenty (years).
3. The (boys) played (soccer) while the (girls) played (baseball).
4. Jenny and her (friend) Susan were in the school (play), A Christmas Story.
5. Don't step in the (puddle) by the bottom (step).
6. The CN Tower is one of the tallest (structures) in North America.
7. Mr. Jones travelled to England and visited Buckingham Palace.
8. We travelled across Europe by (train).

C.
1. famous
2. unsuspecting
3. classification
4. extinct
5. distinct
6. broad
7. powerful
8. developed
9. domestic
10. methods
11. stalk
12. popular

2 The "Horseless Carriage" (1)

A.
1. F
2. F
3. F
4. O
5. O
6. F
7. O
8. F
9. O
10. F
11. F
12. F

B. (Answers will vary.)

C.
1. N
2. A
3. A
4. A ; A
5. A
6. N
7. N
8. A
9. A
10. A

D. (Answers will vary.)

E.
1. inspired
2. capable
3. paved
4. critics
5. invention
6. imagine
7. development
8. perfected
9. bicycle
10. improvement
11. successful
12. powered
13. suburbs
14. mechanics

3 The "Horseless Carriage" (2)

A.
1. Assembly line production was introduced.
2. Henry Ford used the assembly line method to produce cars.
3. More cars were produced.
4. Ford paid his workers $5 a day.
5. Buyers wanted the latest model.
6. The "payment plan" was introduced.

B.
1. T ; (lined) ; the parade route
2. T ; (watched) ; the parade
3. T ; (wore) ; bright costumes
4. I ; (played)
5. T ; (gave) ; candy
6. I ; (smiled)
7. I ; (lasted)
8. I ; (stayed)
9. T ; (tossed) ; fiery torches
10. T ; (filled) ; the sky
11. I ; (smiled)
12. I ; (started) ; (ended)

C.

4 Influenza – More Than Just a Cold

A.
1. flu
2. fever
3. appetite
4. pneumonia
5. 25
6. 5
7. Antibiotics
8. vaccines
9. CDC
10. shots
11. elderly
12. illnesses

B. (Suggested answers)
1. The biggest problem the medical community faces today is that flu strains are constantly changing.
2. The elderly and people with chronic illnesses are most at risk because they are often too weak to fight off the disease.

ISBN: 978-1-897457-05-4

C. 1. D 2. D 3. I 4. I
    5. D 6. D 7. I 8. I
D. 1. bicycle 2. hill
    3. he 4. top
    5. drink 6. trip
    7. way 8. bottom
E. 1. accept 2. edition
    3. altar 4. adept
    5. berth 6. council
    7. Lay 8. minor
    9. role 10. stationery ; stationary

5 Treasures of the Orient (1)

A. 1. T 2. F 3. F 4. T
    5. F 6. T 7. F 8. T
    9. T 10. F 11. F 12. T
B. (Suggested answers)
    1. They wanted to find a quicker and less difficult trade route. The land route was mountainous and time-consuming.
    2. The Europeans could offer manufactured goods for trade in the Orient.
C. 1. They 2. He
    3. We 4. She
D. 1. me ; Indirect 2. him ; Direct
    3. him ; Indirect 4. him ; Direct
    5. her ; Indirect
E. 1. channelled • • A. cost
    2. established • • B. to ask for
    3. expense • • C. sent in one direction
    4. excursion • • D. heritage
    5. objective • • E. encouraged
    6. request • • F. made, developed
    7. culture • • G. trip
    8. inspired • • H. purpose
F. (Individual writing)

6 Treasures of the Orient (2)

A. (Suggested answers)
    1. They could sell goods that were not available in Europe such as silk and spices.
    2. The route around Africa was already of interest to many countries. Those who believed that the world was round thought that an alternate and perhaps safer and quicker route might be found by sailing west.
    3. There were great riches in the Americas. Also it was the discovery of an entire continent that could be claimed and later settled by the Spanish.
    4. Yes. He discovered the Grand Banks that even today stands as one of the richest fishing areas in the world.

    5. Magellan officially completed the journey to the Pacific Ocean.
    6. (Answer will vary.)
    7. (Answer will vary.)
B. 1. their 2. his ; his
    3. our 4. your
    5. her 6. my
C. 1. who 2. which
    3. that 4. whom
D. 1. routes 2. dispute
    3. profit 4. exotic
    5. voyage
E. (Individual writing)

7 Gypsies – an Endangered Culture

A. (Suggested answers)
    Paragraph One – The Gypsies are one of the many cultural groups that face extinction.
    Paragraph Two – Gypsies are a nomadic culture that make a living by doing many different types of work.
    Paragraph Three – The Eastern European Gypsies had a different lifestyle from those in Western Europe.
    Paragraph Four – Gypsies have assimilated with many other cultures but in many countries they are neither trusted nor welcome.
B. 1. Gypsies are often thought of as dishonest traders.
    2. Many Gypsies have assimilated with other cultures and given up their own cultural characteristics.
    3. They wore bright, colourful clothing.
C. 1. The long train slowly crossed the highway delaying all the cars.
    2. The happy child enthusiastically opened her Christmas gifts.
    3. The disappointed children sat quietly at their desks.
    4. A loud voice rang out from the crowd.
    5. The rock band played loudly for their devoted fans.
D. (Individual writing)
E. 1. spacious 2. stormy
    3. thrilled 4. scampered
    5. delicious
F. 1. stormy 2. howled
    3. tightly 4. terrified
    5. flashed 6. booming
    7. poured 8. abandoned
    9. patiently 10. subside
    11. gleamed 12. skipped
    13. arrived 14. drenched
    15. steaming

ISBN: 978-1-897457-05-4

8 The Amazing Helen Keller (1)

A. 1. B   2. C   3. A   4. A
    5. B   6. C

B. 1. The boys and girls|played in the yard.
    2. Cats and dogs|are not always friends.
    3. Morning|is my favourite time of day.
    4. The wind|howled through the night.
    5. Summer holidays|will be here soon.

C. 1. ⟨Getting⟩ to school on time <u>was</u> impossible for him.
    2. The ⟨team⟩ <u>arrived</u> late for their game.
    3. The ⟨waves⟩ <u>crashed</u> to the shore in the wind.
    4. ⟨Happiness⟩ <u>is</u> eating ice cream.
    5. Track and field ⟨athletes⟩ <u>are</u> a special breed.

D. (Answers will vary.)

E. (Suggested answers)
    1. smiled   2. whistled
    3. protected   4. waved
    5. laughed

9 The Amazing Helen Keller (2)

A. 1. The day that Helen ... point in her life.
    2. Helen Keller completed ... seven in all.
    3. This play was made ... in 1962.
    4. She was determined ... Commission for the Blind.
    5. Anne, who was ... using this method.
    6. At the age of twenty ... four years later.
    7. Remarkably, she specialized ... and philosophy.
    8. She toured England ... of the handicapped.

B. 1. The ⟨children⟩ <u>bought</u> the candy at the store.
    2. The racing ⟨cars⟩ <u>roared</u> around the track.
    3. <u>Be</u> careful of slipping on the ice.
    4. The hungry ⟨boy⟩ <u>ate</u> the steaming hot pizza.
    5. The colourful ⟨sailboat⟩ <u>drifted</u> across the calm water.

C. 1. appropriate   2. kind
    3. spell   4. ability
    5. firm   6. complete

D. 1. helpful   2. impossible
    3. lovable   4. inform / formation
    5. unafraid   6. nervous
    7. movable   8. unclear
    9. disagree / agreeable
    10. disprove / improve / provable
    11. truthful   12. famous
    13. increase   14. intend

Progress Test 1

A. 1. A   2. D   3. D   4. B
    5. A   6. C   7. B   8. D
    9. B   10. B   11. C   12. C
    13. C   14. C   15. D   16. C
    17. C   18. A   19. C   20. C

B. 1. flowers ; T   2. fly ; T
    3. I   4. arena ; T
    5. ball ; T

C. 1. She ; S   2. her ; D
    3. him ; D   4. They ; S
    5. him ; I

D. 1. his   2. our
    3. their   4. her
    5. your   6. whom
    7. which   8. who

E. It was a <u>cold</u> and <u>windy</u> <u>winter</u> morning. The <u>frozen</u> streets were ⟨dangerously⟩ <u>slippery</u>. The <u>delivery</u> truck moved ⟨slowly⟩ down the <u>icy</u> street stopping ⟨cautiously⟩ in front of the <u>grocery</u> store. The driver stepped ⟨gently⟩ onto the sidewalk and held the <u>car</u> door ⟨tightly⟩, ⟨cleverly⟩ avoiding a slip on the first step.

F. 1. The ⟨cat⟩ <u>chased</u> the dog around the yard.
    2. The ⟨moon⟩ <u>shone</u> brightly in the night sky.
    3. ⟨Happiness⟩ <u>is</u> skiing down a mountain.
    4. ⟨He⟩ <u>fell</u> down on the slippery road.
    5. The ⟨students⟩ <u>cheered</u> their track and field team to victory.

G. (Suggested answers)
    1. His favourite sports were hockey and soccer.
    2. The sky was blue and the water was calm.
    3. Awards were given out on the last day of school.
    4. He waited inside the shelter for the rain to stop.

H. 1. broad   2. extinct
    3. stalk   4. exotic
    5. critical   6. domestic
    7. excursion   8. objective
    9. inspired   10. unsuspecting

I. 1. impossible   2. successful
    3. incomplete   4. transportation
    5. unfair   6. reasonable
    7. famous   8. disappear

J. 1. enormous   2. attractive
    3. agreeable   4. swift
    5. extensive   6. towering
    7. hazardous   8. fluffy
    9. firm   10. exit
    11. steaming   12. stroll
    13. scurried   14. strike

K. (Suggested answers)
    1. The ferocious dog barked loudly.
    2. The speedy girls ran swiftly.
    3. The happy crowd yelled cheerfully.

10 Mae Jemison – a Great Inspiration

A. 1. O   2. F   3. F   4. O
    5. O   6. O   7. F   8. O
    9. F   10. F

B. (Answers will vary.)

C. 1. caring   2. helping
   3. determined   4. exciting
   5. stimulating   6. selected
   7. challenging ; exhausted
D. (Individual writing)
E. 1. Singing   2. Exploring
   3. helping   4. Giving ; receiving
   5. Becoming   6. swimming ; hiking
   7. acting
F. 1. participle   2. gerund
   3. participle   4. gerund
   5. participle   6. gerund
   7. participle

11 Who Is the Greatest Hockey Player of All Time?

A. 1a. Wayne Gretzky
   b. Gordie Howe
   2. Orr made end-to-end rushes with the puck.
   3a. the MVP
   b. the leading point scorer
   c. the best defenseman
   d. the play-off MVP
   4. He had serious knee problems.
   5. He was named the tournament MVP.
   6. He was a rushing defenseman who was high scoring.
B. (Answers will vary.)
C. 1. threw ; will throw
   2. win ; will win
   3. began ; will begin
   4. come ; will come
   5. did ; will do
   6. think ; thought
   7. fought ; will fight
   8. lost ; will lose
   9. wear ; will wear
   10. wrote ; will write
   11. grow ; will grow
   12. shake ; shook
D. 1. lovely   2. creative
   3. helpful   4. useful
   5. carelessness   6. fortunate
   7. given   8. decision
   9. tightened   10. multiplication ; division
E. (Order may vary.)
scoring / scorer ; traditionally ; occasionally ; believe ; distinguishing ; milestones ; himself ; furiously ; speculation ; operations ; successful ; exciting

12 Bicycles – Then and Now

A.

1. safety bicycle		A. resembled a tricycle
2. modern bicycle		B. safety bicycle was designed
3. Tour de France		C. ratio of gears
4. velocipede		D. reason for today's use
5. 1887		E. shifts the chain
6. 32 teeth		F. international race
7. 8 teeth		G. front chainwheel
8. 4 to 1		H. smaller front wheel
9. environmental concerns		I. fast, durable, comfortable
10. derailer		J. rear chainwheel

B. (Answers will vary.)
C. 1. is   2. She
   3. told   4. rang ; went
   5. were   6. play
   7. rings ; come   8. were
   9. speak   10. were
   11. chose ; preferred   12. took
D. 1. FAMOUS   2. LEVELS
   3. REDUCING   4. ROTATIONS
   5. PROPULSION   6. SAFETY
   7. RENEWED   8. DURABLE
   9. DIFFERENT   10. COMFORTABLE

13 Marilyn Bell – Marathon Swimmer (1)

A. 1. O   2. F
   3. F   4. F
   5. F   6. F
   7. O   8. F
   9. F   10. O
   11. O   12. F
B. (Answers will vary.)
C. 1. Winter in Canada can be cold but some areas of the country are colder than others.
   2. They played on the same basketball team.
   3. The choir sang at the graduation ceremony.
   4. The wild animals in the zoo were caged.
   5. Because it was a hot day, they swam in the public swimming pool nearby.
D. (Individual writing)
E. (Individual writing)

14 Marilyn Bell – Marathon Swimmer (2)

A. 1. T   2. F
   3. T   4. T
   5. F   6. F
   7. F   8. T
   9. T   10. F
   11. T   12. T
B. (Answers will vary.)

C.　1.　Adv.　　　　2.　Adv.
　　3.　Adj.　　　　4.　Adj.
　　5.　Adv.　　　　6.　Adv.
　　7.　Adj.　　　　8.　Adv.
　　9.　Adj.　　　　10.　Adv.
D.　(Individual writing)
E.　(Individual writing)

15　Meat-Eating Plants

A.　1.　carnivorous　　2.　insects
　　3.　diet　　　　　　4.　Venus Flytrap
　　5.　Sticky Sundew　6.　nectar
　　7.　confused　　　　8.　enzymes
　　9.　weeks　　　　　10.　wind
　　11.　exoskeleton
B.　(Answers will vary.)
C.　1.　Whenever I run too fast
　　2.　After we played the game
　　3.　because it was an emergency
　　4.　as long as he wanted
　　5.　Even if they had tried harder
　　6.　as the sun set
　　7.　as if no one could see what he was doing
　　8.　Although the students were well-behaved
　　9.　while she waited for her friend to call
　　10.　as soon as he got the message
　　11.　even though we were not the champions
　　12.　since I wasn't there
　　13.　before I could take a photo of it
D.

b	o	w	p	r	e	d	a	t	o	r	d
e	k	o	l	t	z	r	m	s	b	y	i
k	c	c	p	s	f	a	x	w	j	u	e
r	o	s	u	p	p	l	e	m	e	n	t
u	n	h	g	r	p	i	q	e	j	u	a
l	f	n	c	e	a	g	r	h	e	s	r
x	u	n	s	y	d	h	u	c	v	u	y
p	s	e	c	r	e	t	e	a	g	a	p
j	e	n	t	w	e	s	b	u	e	l	u
a	d	o	r	n	m	e	n	t	s	q	s
n	g	d	e	v	o	u	r	e	d	m	k
w	c	r	a	f	t	i	v	y	o	r	e

E.　(Individual writing)

16　Pirates of the Caribbean (1)

A.　1.　B　　　　　2.　A
　　3.　B　　　　　4.　B
　　5.　A　　　　　6.　B
B.　(Individual writing)

C.
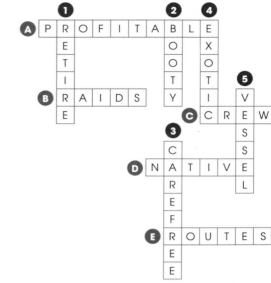

17　Pirates of the Caribbean (2)

A.　1.　They became legendary … North America.
　　2.　Piracy was taking … countries.
　　3.　He was tall … his chest.
　　4.　In one case … evil he was.
　　5.　It was acts … easy for him.
　　6.　A British naval … North Carolina inlet.
　　7.　They then fought … killed him.
　　8.　However, the governor … pounds.
　　9.　With Blackbeard's death came the end of piracy.
　　10.　This paltry payment … risking the lives.
B.　1.　The injured man called for Dr. Smith to come to his aid.
　　2.　The Earl of Sandwich became famous for his invention of the sandwich.
　　3.　The Mona Lisa is one of da Vinci's most famous paintings.
　　4.　Lisa Moore attended the University of Toronto and received a degree in English.
　　5.　She asked, "What time will Professor Higgins give his speech about Pioneers of the Wild West?"
　　6.　The Japanese family arrived in New York on American Airlines and stayed at the Hilton Hotel in upper Manhattan.
C.　(Individual writing)

18　The Origins of Written Words

A.　Paragraph One : A
　　Paragraph Two : B
　　Paragraph Three : B
　　Paragraph Four : A
B.　4 ; 5 ; 1 ; 2 ; 3

ISBN: 978-1-897457-05-4

C.
1. Where would one go to find good weather, interesting shopping, friendly people, and inexpensive accommodations?
2. Why do certain sports such as hockey, golf, and tennis cost so much to play?
3. Hand in your test papers, your special pencils, and your question sheets now.
4. "Get out of bed right now or you'll be late for school," my mother yelled. "Don't you realize it's September 5, the first day of school?"
5. John's father, Mr. Williams, carried the balls, the bases, and the bats.
6. When Susan went shopping at the local store, she bought milk, bread, cheese, eggs, and butter.

D. (Suggested answers)
(Individual writing of meanings)
1. ineffective
2. civilization
3. procession
4. sociable
5. symbolize
6. systematic
7. evolution
8. creative
9. confusing
10. specification

Progress Test 2

A.
1.	B	2.	C
3.	A	4.	C
5.	C	6.	C
7.	A	8.	C
9.	C	10.	B
11.	A	12.	C
13.	B		

B.
1. go
2. won
3. told
4. were ; finish
5. came ; lined ; take
6. was ; went

C.
1. squeaking
2. rotten
3. confusing
4. uninvited
5. telling
6. Talking
7. lost

D. (Answers will vary.)
E. (Individual writing)
F.
1. "Is it cold outside?" she asked.
2. Sam's birthday was August 15, 1989.
3. "Stop! Don't move," shouted the police officer.
4. Dr. Smith worked for the Canadian Ministry of Health.
5. The small, frightened Siamese cat curled up in her lap.
6. On a recent trip to Toronto, his family went to watch the Blue Jays.

G.
1. running
2. rises ; sets
3. satisfied
4. completed
5. guaranteed
6. replaceable
7. difference
8. swiftly ; defeated ; runner
9. sewed ; washed ; hung

H.
1.

```
      C
      R
      A
S P E C U L A T E
      A
      T
      E
```

2.

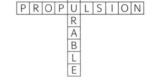

```
        E
        X
P R O C E S S
        I
        T
        E
```

3.

```
        D
P R O P U L S I O N
        R
        A
        B
        L
        E
```

4.

```
                    F
D I S T I N G U I S H
                    R
                    I
                    O
                    U
                    S
```

5.

```
        S
E V O L V E D
        C
        I
        A
        L
```

6.

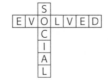

```
        P
        R
M A S T E R E D
        D
        A
        T
        O
        R
```

ISBN: 978-1-897457-05-4

1　Nouns

A.　1. G　　　　　2. F
　　3. B　　　　　4. H
　　5. A　　　　　6. I
　　7. C　　　　　8. D
　　9. E　　　　　10. J

B.　2. Atlantis ; P　　　3. one ; CC
　　4. mysteries ; CC　　5. island ; CC
　　6. Atlantic Ocean ; CP　7. day ; CC
　　8. night ; CC　　　10. detail ; UC
　　12. philosopher ; CC　13. Poseidon ; P
　　14. Zeus ; P　　　15. Life ; UC
　　16. generations ; CC　17. people ; CC
　　18. story ; CC　　　19. lesson ; CC
　　20. way ; CC

　　9. years ; CC
　　11. Plato ; P

C.　1. D　　　　　2. D
　　3. I　　　　　4. D
　　5. I

D.　1. D　　　　　2. I
　　3. D ; I　　　　4. D
　　5. D ; I　　　　6. N
　　7. D　　　　　8. N

E.　Direct Objects:
　　snack ; bottom of the staircase ; mouse ; creeps ; feeling ;
　　something ; wisp of air ; house ; wind ; cat ; cape ; cabinet
　　Indirect Objects:
　　her ; her ; home

2　Pronouns

A.　Subject pronouns: 4 ; 5 ; 6
　　Object pronouns: 1 ; 7
　　Reflexive pronouns: 2 ; 3 ; 8

B.　1. myself　　　　2. himself
　　3. herself　　　　4. themselves
　　5. ourselves

C.　1. It　　　　　2. me
　　3. I　　　　　4. you
　　5. They

D.　1. these　　　　2. this
　　3. That　　　　4. ones
　　5. ones　　　　6. this
　　7. that　　　　8. Those

E.　1. that　　　　2. where
　　3. which　　　　4. whose
　　5. when　　　　6. whom
　　7. that　　　　8. who

3　Verbs (1)

A.　1. A
　　2. A
　　3. P
　　4. A
　　5. P
　　6. A
　　7. P
　　8. A

B.　Ability: 2 ; 5 ; 6
　　Permission: 3 ; 4
　　Possibility: 1 ; 7 ; 8

C.　(Suggested writing)
　　1. Could you turn the stereo down a bit, please?
　　2. Will you pick up a few cartons from the store?
　　3. Could you pick up the phone for me, please?
　　4. Would you help me open the windows?

D.　(Individual writing)

4　Verbs (2)

A.　1. is showing
　　2. are running
　　3. is blowing
　　4. is chewing
　　5. is going
　　6. are preparing
　　7. is simmering
　　8. is shining
　　9. is burning

B.　1. sings
　　2. is thinking
　　3. looks
　　4. likes
　　5. is planning
　　6. am arriving
　　7. reads
　　8. gives

C.　(Suggested writing)
　　1a. The farmers milk their cows every day.
　　b. The farmers are milking their cows now.
　　2a. The children lie in the meadow every afternoon.
　　b. The children are lying in the meadow.
　　3a. Daphne and Sophia fall asleep in front of the television every night.
　　b. Daphne and Sophia are falling asleep in front of the television.

D.　1. was flying　　　2. talked
　　3. was walking　　4. was rehearsing
　　5. played　　　　6. was taking
　　7. had　　　　　8. spotted ; decided

ISBN: 978-1-897457-05-4

E. 1. will watch
    2. will ring
    3. will be visiting
    4. will be
    5. will be riding
    6. will be attending
    7. will play
    8. will be swimming
    9. will drive

5 Verbs (3)

A. 1. active
    2. passive
    3. passive
    4. active
    5. passive
    6. active
    7. active
    8. passive
    9. passive
    10. active
B. 2. Charmaine's hair was tied with ribbons.
    3. Charmaine's bag was checked.
    4. The airplane was boarded.
    5. The passengers were shown their seats.
    6. Charmaine's bag was put in the overhead compartment.
    7. The overhead compartments were filled with more bags.
    8. The seats were placed in upright positions.
    9. The plane was prepared for take-off.
C. 1. unfastened the seatbelts
    2. served passengers light snacks on the plane
    3. told the passengers there would be a delay
    4. occupied the washrooms yet
    5. gave Charmaine some paper and crayons
    6. drew a cute airplane
    7. asked the passengers if they would like a drink
    8. handed out newspapers
    9. could see clouds through the windows
    10. gave Charmaine a choice of meals
D. 2. The passengers were handed some extra napkins.
    3. A movie was shown to the passengers.
    4. The passengers were given earphones for the audio system.
    5. The passengers were told the safety precautions.
    6. The weather report was provided to the passengers.
    7. The passengers were offered desserts and drinks.
    8. Charmaine was handed the bag after the plane had landed.

6 Adjectives and Adverbs

A. 1. safer ; safest
    2. happier
    3. most forgetful
    4. greater ; greatest
    5. biggest
    6. friendlier ; friendliest
    7. sadder ; saddest
    8. nicer ; nicest
    9. more important
    10. thinner ; thinnest
    11. more influential ; most influential
    12. easier ; easiest
    13. tinier ; tiniest
    14. more marvellous ; most marvellous
B. 1. tidiest
    2. most splendid
    3. ✔
    4. ✔
    5. happiest
    6. more fun
C. 1. Doris thinks Toronto is the most bustling city in Canada.
    2. Jack/Jill is a more careful person than Jill/Jack.
    3. Kelly/Dana is usually faster than Dana/Kelly.
    4. Rome/Paris is a more beautiful city than Paris/Rome.
    5. Judy is the tallest girl in class.
D. 1. charming ; charmed
    2. annoying ; annoyed
    3. frightening ; frightened
    4. embarrassing ; embarrassed
    5. boring ; bored
    6. welcoming ; welcomed
    7. moving ; moved
E. 1. frightened
    2. bored
    3. annoying
    4. charming
    5. moving
F. 1. later   2. sooner
    3. more frequently   4. the earliest
    5. most often   6. more usually

Progress Test 1

A. (Underline these countable common nouns.)
    vacation ; son ; daughter ; family ; vacations ; time
    car ; item ; tent ; bags ; pillows ; games ; cooler
    car ; house ; times ; games ; movies
    trip
    (Circle these uncountable common nouns.)
    clothing ; gear ; repellent ; sunscreen ; water
    time
    fun

B. 1. The Garcias
    2. Mr. Garcia
    3. Mrs. Garcia
    4. Ivan
    5. Marissa
    6. Sandbanks Provincial Park
    7. Ontario
    8. Sandbanks Provincial Park
C. 1. D
    2. D
    3. I
    4. I
    5. D
    6. I
    7. D
    8. D
D. 1. which
    2. He
    3. him
    4. this
    5. we
    6. us
    7. They
    8. herself
    9. she
    10. themselves
E. 1. can
    2. could
    3. could
    4. cannot
    5. Can
    6. can't
    Ability: 2 ; 4 ; 5
    Permission: 1 ; 6
    Possibility: 3
F. 1. Ivan and Marissa are walking along the beach.
    2. The wind is blowing gently.
    3. Ivan is wearing his sandals.
    4. Marissa is wishing she could watch a movie.
    5. Ivan is thinking about his favourite video game.
G. 1. will be feeling
    2. will rest
    3. suggests
    4. were running
    5. saw
H. 1. active
    2. active
    3. passive
    4. active
    5. passive
    6. active
    7. passive

I. 1. faster
    2. most interesting
    3. prettier
    4. shiniest
    5. sillier
    6. most popular
    7. more important

7 Conjunctions

A. 1. and ; before
    2. until
    3. after
    4. unless
    5. or
    6. if
    7. Although
    8. because
    9. since
    10. and
B. 1. because
    2. but
    3. unless
    4. Although ; still
    5. if
    6. when
    7. therefore
    8. so
C. 1. not only ; but also
    2. Either ; or
    3. both ; and
    4. whether ; or
    5. neither ; nor
    6. whether ; or
    7. not only ; but also
    8. neither ; nor
    9. both ; and
D. (Suggested answers)
    1. You can run but you can't hide.
    2. Maggie will meet us at the skating rink since it is close to her house.
    3. Tristan didn't finish his homework last night so he won't be able to go to the fair with us.
    4. The blue team didn't win although they put forth their best effort.
    5. Darryl didn't like the restaurant so next time, he will eat somewhere else.
    6. Mrs. Bryant bought three packages of cookies because they were on sale.
    7. Allison and Peter didn't like the restaurant but they are going to give it another try.
    8. Hiking in the woods is fun and it is also good for you.

8 Phrases

A. 1. S
2. C
3. O
4. C
5. C
6. O
7. O
8. S

B. Adjective Phrases: 1 ; 5 ; 6 ; 8
Adverb Phrases: 2 ; 3 ; 4 ; 7

C. 1. to go to the amusement park
2. to be among the first in line for their rides
3. to ride on the roller-coaster
4. to try the Swing of the Millennium
5. to get some food
6. to ride on the carousel
7. to look at the design
8. to sit down on
9. to share some French fries with Rachel and Kim

D. 1. P
2. O
3. C
4. S

E. 1. playing sports of all kinds
2. Biting nails
3. Forgiving your siblings
4. waiting for her turn

9 Clauses

A. 1. D
2. I
3. D
4. I
5. I
6. I
7. I
8. D
9. D
10. I

B. (Individual writing)
C. (Individual writing)
D. 1. adv
2. adj
3. adv
4. adv
5. adv
6. adv
7. adj

8. adv
9. adj
10. adj
11. adv
12. adv

E. (Individual writing)
F. (Individual writing)

10 Sentences

A. 1.
2. ✔
3. ✔
4.
5.
6. ✔
7.
8. ✔
9. ✔
10.

B. (Individual writing)
C. 1. he wouldn't hurt a flea
2. I have to be home by 5 p.m.
3. I will have to walk to school
4. they are proud of their high marks
5. the teams will play tomorrow
6. we will visit our friends

D. (Individual writing)
E. 1. 2
2. 3
3. 2
4. 2
5. 3

F. Simple: 1 ; 3 ; 4 ; 5
Compound: 7 ; 8
Complex: 2 ; 6

11 Punctuation

A. 1. Samantha, Jacquelyn, and Grace went to the concert together.
2. Kevin, can you please help me?
3. Mom, Dad, and I are going to visit Toronto, Montreal, and Halifax this summer.
4. Pepper, my dog, knows a lot of tricks.
5. "I am going for a walk," said Taylor.
6. He wore a thick, furry coat because it was cold outside.
7. Dad went to get eggs, milk, cheese, and butter.
8. Natasha likes to play tennis, read, and paint.
9. Toby, please set the table.
10. "We will go to the museum on Sunday," said Gregory.

ISBN: 978-1-897457-05-4

B. 1. Sherry has three items on her birthday list: a telescope, drawing pencils, and a new dress.
   2. There was one problem with Robert's plan: he didn't have enough money to buy the material.
   3. Never take school for granted: some children in poor countries never get the chance to attend.
   4. There are four foods Stephanie doesn't like to eat: beans, pork, salmon, and bananas.
C. 1. Daisy said she will be late for dinner; she has an appointment.
   2. Tomorrow it will rain; it will be good for the garden.
   3. We cannot wait much longer; we will miss our bus.
   4. It is not necessary to bring a gift; it is your presence that is most desired.
   5. She was late for her piano lesson this afternoon; it will never happen again.
   6. Jeremy's backyard is quite large; it is great for running around in.
   7. The last city we visited was Stockholm; it was my favourite.
   8. The Art History test was very difficult; Molly and Keith did quite well.
   9. The Mona Lisa is in Paris; I don't think I will ever see it in person.
   10. He had a difficult time with the yard work; he will ask for help next time.
D. (Individual writing)
E. 1. The cities we will visit – Rome, Paris, and London – will all be very interesting.
   2. Teresa was happy to find out the surprise – a new puppy!
   3. Gavin put on his blue sweater – the one his grandmother knitted for him – before he went outside.
   4. The camp offers a variety of activities – soccer, crafts, swimming, photography, and cooking – so there is something for every kid to enjoy.
F. Ms. Duncan's grade six class went to Kearney for a week-long trip in June. The kids learned a number of things: how to canoe, how to make dream catchers, and how to work in teams. One morning, they stopped by a marsh to learn about insects that live in water. "Let's study these insects," Ms. Duncan said. The camp leaders were glad that every kid had brought insect repellent in tubes; aerosol cans are not good for the environment. Each evening a leader named Mike would teach his kids a new song – one of which was called "The Merry Moose" – so the kids could sing their way back to the cabins afterwards.

12 Writing Paragraphs

A. (Underline these sentences.)
   1. Today, each child in class had to write a riddle and pass it to the person sitting behind him or her. ; Apparently, Jonathan had written a riddle about her, something she would never have expected!
   2. The strap on her left sandal got caught in the pedal and she lost balance. Natalie hurt her knee but luckily, she did not injure her kneecap.
B. (Individual writing)
C. (Individual writing)
D. (Individual writing)

13 Formal and Informal Writing

A. 1.
   2. ✔
   3. ✔
   4.
   5. ✔
   6. ✔
B. (Individual writing)
C. (Individual writing)
D. (Individual writing)
E. (Individual writing)
F. (Individual writing)

Progress Test 2

A. (Circle these conjunctions.)
   and ; and ; and ; before ; and
   and ; after ; and
   or
   after
   and ; but
   unless ; because
   so ; although ; and
B. 1. noun
   2. adverb
   3. noun
   4. adjective
   5. adjective
   6. adverb
C. 1. reading aloud
   2. to know the identity
   3. solving the mystery
   4. to hurry up
   5. to go searching
   6. to look for more clues

D. 1. Marissa gives Ivan the note
    2. He reads the note to himself
    3. Although he already knows what the note says
    4. after they finish eating their breakfast
    5. They are sure they will find more clues

E. 1. adv
    2. adj
    3. adv
    4. adv

F. 1. simple
    2. complex
    3. simple
    4. simple
    5. compound
    6. complex
    7. complex
    8. compound

G. (Suggested answers)

"I just remembered the note!" says Marissa. Ivan and Marissa race back to where they met Tammy. "We forgot to tell you," says Marissa, "we found something inside the bottle – an old note that must belong to your grandmother!" Ivan hands Tammy the note.

"Actually, my friend Carlos wrote that note," Tammy says pointing to the boy standing next to her. "Sorry to disappoint you, but we were just playing."

"We thought it might have belonged to a sailor or a pirate!" says Ivan.

"We were playing something like that," Tammy says. "Would you like to play with us?" Ivan and Marissa are happy she has asked; they decide to stay and play.

H. (Underline these sentences.)
Ivan and Marissa play with Tammy, Carlos, and the other children for the rest of their camping trip.
They have discovered that using their imagination can be a lot more fun than playing computer and video games.

I. (Individual writing)

1 The Topic Sentence

A. 1. C   2. B
    3. A   4. A
B. (Answers will vary.)
C. (Answers will vary.)
D. (Answers will vary.)

2 Following the Topic Sentence

A. (Answers will vary.)
B. (Answers will vary.)
C. (Answers will vary.)

3 Descriptive Language (1)

A. 1. lodge   2. mansion
    3. ferocious   4. (an) interesting
    5. comedian   6. lanky
    7. convertible   8. lighthouse
    9. sprinter   10. gourmet
B. 1. sauntered   2. rushed
    3. leaped   4. swooped
    5. zigzagged   6. slammed
    7. drifted   8. flashed
    9. blazed   10. devoured
C. 1. instantaneous   2. gingerly
    3. roared   4. voyage
    5. precarious   6. refreshing
    7. sleek   8. executed
    9. complications   10. undulating
    11. efficiently   12. floated
    13. gracefully   14. careening
    15. shrieked / roared
D. (Sentences will vary.)
    1. singing   2. dining
    3. running   4. crying
    5. speaking   6. fishing
    7. swimming   8. driving
    9. burning   10. falling

4 Confusing Words

A. 1. noticeable   2. definite
    3. success   4. heroes
    5. occurrence   6. necessary
    7. receive   8. therefore
    9. professor   10. argument

B. 1. their   2. presents
    3. hole   4. passed
    5. Who's   6. sight
    7. weak   8. duel
    9. fourth   10. loose
    11. alter   12. bear
    13. bear   14. herd
    15. patients   16. principal
    17. plane ; plain   18. council ; counsel
    19. hoarse   20. diary
    21. fare ; fair   22. break
    23. peace   24. course
    25. bored
C. 1. this   2. these
    3. This   4. Those
    5. this   6. these
    7. Those   8. them
    9. That
D. 1. good   2. bad
    3. good   4. bad
    5. badly   6. good
E. 1. fewer   2. less
    3. Fewer   4. fewer
    5. less   6. fewer

5 Creating a Story Ending

A. (Answers will vary.)
B. 1. mid-June
    2. located at the track and field meet
C. Major : Lisa, Jennifer
    Minor : the announcer, the starter, other
             competitors, the crowd
D. (Answers will vary.)
    1. The scorching sun blazed down on the competitors.
    2. They arched their backs and lowered their heads.
    3. The crowd cheered wildly.
    4. She stumbled and sprawled.
E. (Answer will vary.)
    This is a story about two highly competitive runners that compete against each other at a championship track meet. While running neck and neck, one of the runners stumbles.
F. (Answer will vary.)
    There is conflict between the two runners, Lisa and Jennifer. There is also conflict between Lisa and herself as she must have the courage to recover from her accident.

G. (Answer will vary.)

The suspense is first built up with the two runners preparing to race. Further suspense is built when the runners are neck and neck after 30 metres into the race. Suspense continues when Lisa stumbles.

H. (Answer will vary.)

6 Word-Building Challenge

A. (Answers will vary.)
1. engagement ; disengage
Best synonym : occupy
2. occurrence ; occurred
Best synonym : happen
3. enrage ; raging
Best synonym : fury
4. production ; producer
Best synonym : make
5. neglectful ; negligence
Best synonym : ignore
6. identified ; identical
Best synonym : self

B. 1. fad
2. individuality
3. omit
4. transpire
5. yield
6. monopolize

C. 1. bearable
2. important
3. incapable
4. disgusting
5. well-known
6. stubborn
7. difficult
8. dangerous
9. incredible
10. pitiful

D. 1 a. stare   b. stair
2 a. core   b. corps
3 a. pores   b. pours
4 a. break   b. brake
5 a. red   b. read
6 a. night   b. knight
7 a. allowed   b. aloud
8 a. rain   b. reign
9 a. way   b. weigh
10 a. sail   b. sale

7 Descriptive Language (2)

A. 1. hazardous
2. glad
3. spacious
4. hideous
5. challenging
6. pace
7. deafening
8. glided
9. dove

B. 1. K
2. L
3. M
4. N
5. O
6. C
7. A
8. F
9. P
10. D
11. E
12. G
13. H
14. I
15. J
16. B

C. (Suggestions only)
1. abundance
2. jeering
3. bleak
4. energetic
5. ornate
6. obstinate
7. obscure
8. consecutive
9. cantankerous
10. grievance
11. intrigued
12. absurd
13. coincidental
14. grimace
15. logical

Progress Test 1

A. 1. C
2. A
3. B
4. B
5. C

B. 1. H
2. I
3. G
4. B
5. C
6. D
7. A
8. J
9. F
10. E

C. 1. F
2. G
3. I
4. B
5. C
6. H
7. D
8. E
9. J
10. A

D. 1. E
2. D
3. A
4. B
5. C
6. B
7. D
8. E
9. C
10. A
11. E
12. C
13. D
14. A
15. B

E. 1. I ; noticeable
2. C
3. I ; therefore
4. I ; necessary
5. I ; receive
6. I ; heroes
7. C
8. C
9. I ; professor
10. I ; occurrence

F. 1. their
2. presence
3. Whose
4. plane

5. herd
7. bored

6. principal
8. fair

G. 1. this
3. well
5. bad
7. less
9. fewer

2. Those
4. good
6. badly
8. less
10. less

H. 1. decide
3. rage
5. neglect

2. occur
4. produce
6. identity

I. 1. C
3. A
5. D
7. J
9. G

2. E
4. I
6. B
8. F
10. H

J. 1. dangerous
3. hideous
5. deafening

2. spacious
4. challenging
6. floated

K. 1. pours
3. red / reed
5. allowed
7. way

2. brake
4. knight
6. reign
8. sale

L. (Answers will vary.)

8 The Columbia Icefield

A. 1. gradual
3. harsh
5. environment
7. approximately
9. boundary
11. establish
13. venture
15. enforced
17. conservation

2. traction
4. breath-taking
6. accessible
8. situated
10. accumulated
12. base
14. detectable
16. designed

B. (Answers will vary.)
Paragraph One :
1. The Columbia Icefield is located on the boundary of Jasper and Banff national parks.
2. The Icefield is 350 metres thick.
Paragraph Two :
1. Tourists take a Snocoach out onto the glacier.
2. The Icefield is made up of falling snow that has accumulated for over 400 years.
Paragraph Three :
1. Grizzly bears have winter dens near the Icefield.
2. Strict rules of conservation are enforced to protect plants and animals.

Paragraph Four :
1. Thousands of people visit the Icefield each year.
2. This region has wildlife, rivers, mountains, and lakes for tourists to enjoy.
C. (Answers will vary.)

9 Haiku Poetry

A. (Answers will vary.)
B. (Answers will vary.)
C. (Answers will vary.)
D. (Answer will vary.)

10 Narrative Writing

A. (Answers will vary.)
B. (Answers will vary.)

11 Vocabulary Development

A. 1. stampede
3. trial
5. cyclist
7. collision
9. captive
11. fixture
13. coincident
15. snowmobile
17. natural
19. automatic

2. relative
4. campsite
6. attraction
8. nonsense
10. victorious
12. repair
14. collection
16. coincidental
18. comical
20. rearrange

B. (Answers will vary.)
1. Mary called her friend on the telephone but she got no answer.
2. As soon as the game was over, everyone went home.
3. If you come over to my house, we can play computer games.
4. The sun came out after the storm was over.
5. He waited for hours for his friends to show up but it started to get dark.
6. When the school bell rang, summer holidays had started.
7. Because he was the team captain, he had to be a leader.
8. After they ate dinner, they had dessert.
9. His new bike was very fast but it was too big for him.

10. Although his alarm went off, he was late for school.
11. Even though they were the first to arrive, they still waited a long time in line.
12. They were camping in the mountains when a bear visited their campsite.

C. (Answers will vary.)

D. (Answers will vary.)

12 Expository Writing

A. (Answers will vary.)
1. To instruct the reader as to the best way to establish a campfire
2. Although sitting around a campfire is one of the great joys of camping, building a long lasting, roaring campfire is not a simple task.
3. At this point you should be enjoying a roaring fire but be mindful to add wood consistently to maintain enough fuel to keep your fire going.

B. (Answers will vary.)
1. To explain to the reader that there are many interesting and fun things to do in the city during the summer
2. However, the city offers a variety of interesting ways to spend the hot, lazy days of summer.
3. Whatever your preference, the city in the summer is a lively place with something for everyone.

Challenge
(Answer will vary.)

C. (Answer will vary.)

D. (Answer will vary.)

13 Le Tour de France

Paragraph One :
1. B   2. A
3. C
(Individual writing of the sentence)
Paragraph Two :
1. B   2. E
3. C   4. D
5. A
(Individual writing of the sentence)
Paragraph Three :
1. D   2. E
3. C   4. A
5. G   6. F
7. H   8. B
(Individual writing of the sentence)

Paragraph Four :
1. C   2. H
3. D   4. A
5. F   6. G
7. E   8. B
(Individual writing of the sentence)
Paragraph Five :
1. E   2. C
3. D   4. B
5. A
(Individual writing of the sentence)

14 Informal Writing

A. (Answer will vary.)

B. (Answer will vary.)

C. (Answer will vary.)

D. (Answers will vary.)

15 Synonyms – Facts about Canada

hoisted – 2 ; establishing – 1 ; sovereignty – 3 ; ceded – 4 ; official – 5

originated – 7 ; officially – 10 ; acknowledged – 8 ; maritime – 6 ; original – 13 ; declared – 9 ; version – 11 ; designed – 14 ; symbol – 12

territory – 18 ; extends – 15 ; expanse – 19 ; astounding – 17 ; remarkably – 16 ; diverse – 20

impressive – 25 ; inception – 24 ; accessible – 26 ; transported – 27 ; employed – 21 ; sector – 22 ; opportunities – 28 ; emerge – 23 ; particularly – 29

density – 31 ; unique – 32 ; Primary – 30 ; unprecedented – 33 ; optimistic – 34

initial – 37 ; prior – 39 ; composer – 41 ; accompany – 42 ; numerous – 38 ; renditions – 40 ; unaltered – 35 ; minor – 36

Progress Test 2

A. 1. located   2. area
   3. bottom   4. nearly
   5. approachable   6. wander
   7. grip   8. earned
   9. slow   10. visible
   11. set up   12. rough

13. surroundings
14. protection
15. applied
16. created

B. (Answers will vary.)

C. 1. state
2. coincide
3. relate
4. attract
5. capture
6. collide
7. sense
8. incidence
9. victory
10. repair

D. (Answers will vary.)
1. He walked home because he missed the school bus.
2. She invited her friends over for a sleepover and they ordered pizza.
3. The game continued although it was raining.
4. She set the table while he cooked hot dogs.
5. As soon as the students were seated at their desks, the teacher began teaching.

E. Group A :
1. I
2. J
3. E
4. C
5. G
6. A
7. H
8. D
9. F
10. B

Group B :
1. G
2. E
3. A
4. I
5. B
6. J
7. C
8. F
9. H
10. D

F. 1. C
2. E
3. B
4. D
5. I
6. H
7. F
8. G
9. A
10. J

G. (Answers will vary.)

H. (Answer will vary.)

ISBN: 978-1-897457-05-4

1.

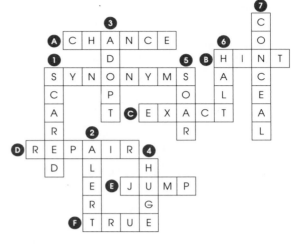

2. (Suggested slides)

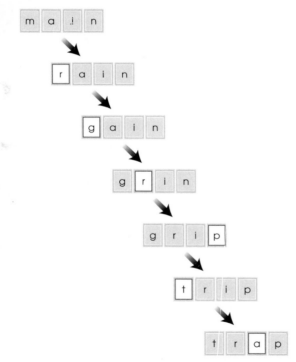

3.

4. (Suggested answers)

D	I	S	H
A			I
R		1	L
T	I	L	L

K	I	N	G
I			A
C		2	T
K	I	T	E

P	E	E	L
O			I
R		3	V
T	A	K	E

H	A	I	R
O			E
P		4	A
E	V	E	R

T	H	A	T
A			I
I		5	C
L	O	O	K

L	I	L	Y
A			A
K		6	R
E	A	R	N

5. WE LIVE ON A PLANET FAR AWAY FROM EARTH. WE WANT TO MAKE NEW FRIENDS. CAN WE BE FRIENDS?

6.

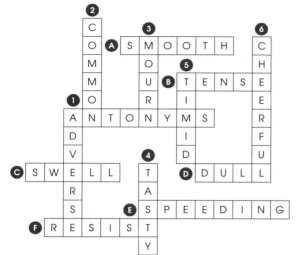

7. (Suggested slides)

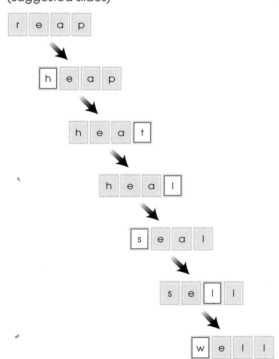

9.

10. 1. honeycomb   2. houseboat
   3. starfish   4. bookworm
   5. firecracker   6. keystone

11.

g	i	r	p	d	o	j	g	t	d	q	s	f	j
k	u	a	x	k	c	l	r	p	e	n	c	i	l
e	r	q	f	n	h	n	i	x	q	b	i	s	k
p	u	l	m	o	s	d	y	q	c	o	s	n	t
c	l	i	p	t	w	m	b	v	z	h	s	a	i
n	e	g	y	e	r	a	s	e	r	q	o	p	r
s	r	o	p	b	a	l	b	p	u	j	r	x	c
d	h	t	j	o	n	x	c	u	z	e	s	m	w
c	r	a	y	o	n	z	t	n	d	y	f	v	t
e	p	y	m	k	i	g	o	c	v	z	r	h	u
k	b	v	s	z	l	v	k	h	b	g	o	n	e
p	i	u	w	h	k	s	t	a	p	l	e	r	m
e	c	m	j	x	w	o	u	l	w	u	j	a	f
n	r	f	y	a	e	s	p	a	p	e	r	q	b

8.

h	c	d	l	f	j	a	n	e	m	g	a	e
f	r	m	g	w	w	h	q	b	a	n	h	b
c	i	c	a	d	a	c	n	s	n	e	j	l
d	c	h	m	o	s	q	u	i	t	o	c	a
m	k	b	o	b	p	e	p	d	i	g	o	d
k	e	p	f	l	b	i	l	g	s	l	c	y
r	t	l	d	j	e	n	f	a	j	c	k	b
c	a	o	v	c	e	u	r	o	t	p	r	u
h	f	c	l	p	t	z	x	i	v	b	o	g
d	b	u	m	b	l	e	b	e	e	i	a	c
a	k	s	e	f	e	i	y	a	m	q	c	i
j	m	t	d	o	q	l	r	m	o	t	h	m
k	a	n	a	n	t	x	b	c	s	r	o	g

12.

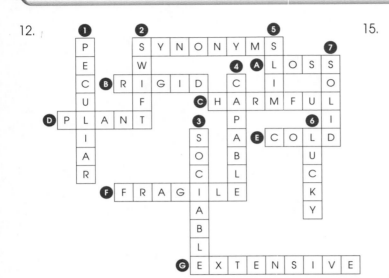

15.

13. (Suggested slides)

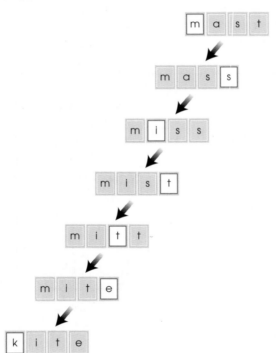

16.

l	n	p	h	d	i	b	g	r	q	y	p	e	n
x	f	H	m	a	e	z	s	w	o	l	u	h	o
c	t	a	n	m	c	H	a	m	h	z	m	j	c
o	b	k	j	y	p	l	n	x	w	i	p	u	g
s	h	d	g	m	o	j	t	r	i	c	k	g	t
t	k	a	w	h	e	q	r	e	l	q	i	H	a
u	H	a	l	l	o	w	e	e	n	t	n	m	k
m	d	f	z	t	p	s	a	y	i	p	q	w	f
e	o	h	t	l	c	n	t	w	s	b	a	e	j
s	p	i	d	e	r	h	s	g	i	a	c	x	o
b	f	n	y	q	s	k	e	l	e	t	o	n	m
p	j	f	x	l	b	z	k	x	d	s	c	p	r
d	z	w	a	r	c	i	g	b	r	f	z	h	l
m	l	x	i	q	j	n	p	o	m	k	y	m	k

14. I dreamt that I skied with Santa Claus last night.

ISBN: 978-1-897457-05-4